FUNDAMENTALLY
SPEAKING

FUNDAMENTALLY
SPEAKING

Henry S. Myers, Jr.

 Strawberry Hill Press

Strawberry Hill Press
616 44th Avenue
San Francisco, California 94121

Distributed by Stackpole Books
Cameron & Kelker Streets
Harrisburg, Pennsylvania 17105

First printing, August, 1977

Manufactured in the United States of America

Library of Congress Cataloging in Publication Data

Myers, Henry S
    Fundamentally speaking.

    Bibliography: p.
    Includes index.
    1. Myers, Henry S. 2. Education--Philosophy.
3. School discipline. 4. Education--United States--
1965-   I. Title.
LB885.M9F86 1977   370'.973   77-3072
ISBN 0-89407-007-X pbk.

To my wife Elizabeth and to my daughters, Tricia, Pam and Judy whose dedication, sacrifice and advice made the Fundamental School possible. And to the memory of my son Butch, Henry Slagle Myers, IV, whose short eleven year stay on this earth continues to inspire and guide me daily.

CONTENTS

I
THE PROBLEM

It's easy to be an alarmist. In fact preaching gloom these days seems to be the "in" thing. From pollution to politics we are told the world is doomed, and such may indeed be true. Unfortunately, however, alarmism has become so widespread that many Americans are beginning to regard it in the category of crying wolf. No matter how frightening the statistics, we shrug our shoulders, puff our cigarettes, drive our gas-gulping automobiles, consume our resources, pollute our environment, and figure that somehow "science" will come to the rescue before it is too late. Why worry? America is the richest, most powerful, and best educated nation in the world. We'll find a way. We always have.

And you know, it's hard to rebut such reasoning. Look at the record. Always in the past, just when times looked the darkest, American ingenuity, American free enterprise, and American hard work and dedication have succeeded in snatching victory out of the jaws of defeat. Will we not be able to do so again? Yes, although others are not so optimistic, I think we can. But first we must understand the problem.

There are, of course, many problems. But none so vital and none so basic as that which permeates our education system. All over the United States that system is in a shambles. You've heard the horror stories. Unfortunately most of them are true. Let me repeat just a few.

THE ILLITERACY INVASION

Each year more than a million high school juniors and seniors all across the country take Scholastic Aptitude Tests — the so-called SAT tests. For ten years straight the average score has been dropping. It is now down 35 points. On the international scene, when American youngsters are compared with the youth of nine European countries, American fourteen-year-olds are in the top four, but our ten-year-olds show up next to last.

This year it was reported that 52 percent of the entering freshmen at the University of California are forced to take "bonehead English" because they cannot write a coherent paragraph. This statistic is even more frightening when coupled with the fact that only the top twelve percent of the high school graduating class is eligible for admission. The cream of the crop.

At the end of the 1974 school year, at one of our junior high schools in Pasadena, I checked the achievement test scores of the eighth graders who were scheduled to graduate into high school. Out of 144 eighth grade students, 25 were achieving at the fourth grade level or lower in reading and mathematics. At our high schools this year, fully 30 percent of our students are programmed into "proficiency" math classes designed for those who cannot perform the simple functions of addition, subtraction, multiplication and division.

The other day a nice looking young girl clerk at one of our local hamburger stands was faced with the problem of giving me change. My bill was 81 cents. I gave her a dollar bill. Eventually I got my correct change, but the poor girl's efforts were pitiful to behold. I'm certain that she was well informed on set theory. She probably also knew how to count in base 2 or base 7. But she couldn't add or subtract. And I'll wager that she was even worse at multiplication and division. Unfortunately the plight of this girl is not an isolated instance. And our generation — not hers — is to blame for her dilemma.

My wife tells the story about a visit to a high-class thrift shop operated by a well-known ladies service club. She browsed a bit and eventually purchased several items for a total cost of $4.77. Automatically she handed the well-dressed volunteer clerk a five dollar bill — plus two pennies. The young lady almost came unglued! "Don't give me those pennies," she pleaded. "I simply can't handle that." My wife just couldn't resist and said, "Oh, you must have attended our public schools." "No," the lady replied, "I went to private school."

Yes, it is easy to become an alarmist. In the first year that our Fundamental School in Pasadena was opened we received more than 500 inquiries from concerned parents, teachers, administrators, and school-board members — from nearly every state in the union, including Alaska. Always the story is the same. "Our children aren't learning anything," they say. "They can't read." "They can't write." "They can't perform the simplest functions of mathematics." "Please give us complete details about your Fundamental School," they plead. "We simply must start one in our community."

The implication is frightening. Think about it. As mortals, our only known method of survival is for each generation to transmit its store of accumulated knowledge to each succeeding generation. If this transmission process becomes inefficient, any nation, no matter how rich, how powerful, or how highly educated she may be at the moment, will ultimately deteriorate and die. Remember, each one of us has only one generation, or possibly two, to work with. If we fail to teach our children or our grandchildren what we know, that portion of our knowledge which we fail to transmit will simply become lost. There is no second chance.

THE SLOB SYNDROME

Not too many years ago we Americans were a proud people with strong convictions. Some of us still are. But slobism today is becoming a national epidemic. And I don't mean simply the growing numbers of long-haired hippies wandering about aimlessly and irresponsibly. They are, of course, one manifestation of the disease, a relatively minor one. Far more serious is the less obvious but infinitely more infectious stage of the malady that is spreading like wildfire, particularly among our youth. And we, the older generations, are both kindling and fanning the flames.

The teaching of pride and respect is just as important for national survival as is the teaching of the three R's. Pride in oneself. Pride in one's school. Pride in one's community. And yes, pride in one's country. Unfortunately this part of our educational curricula is almost nonexistent in many of our public schools today.

Have you visited any of the campuses recently? The high schools are particularly bad, but I have seen advanced stages of the disease even in our kindergartens. Litter and trash everywhere. Soda straws. Candy wrappers. Milk cartons. Lunch sacks. All strewn thoughtlessly about. Grafitti on the walls. Restrooms almost unusable. What a way to bring up our children — to teach them pride — to teach them respect.

And then take a look at the teachers and the administrators. Are they neat, clean, and tidy? Impeccably dressed? Does their very appearance command respect? Does their bearing and their manner reflect pride in their profession? Sometimes it does. But all too often they look like slobs.

There are, of course, varying degrees of slobism. I've seen them all right here in our local school system. And I'll bet many of you have too, in your own home town. The slob-slobs attire themselves in faded blue jeans and sloppy sweatshirts. A great costume, mind you, for digging in the garden on Saturday afternoon. But hardly the garb for a professional teacher on the job. To complete the outfit, thonged sandals sans socks on the feet, and a medallion around the neck. The hair? I won't even go into that.

At this point the antennae of any slob defenders who happen to read this treatise are wagging violently. "It doesn't matter how a person dresses," they argue. "It's only what's inside that counts." Nonsense! Clothes do make the man, and don't let anyone tell you otherwise. Admittedly a teacher's dress, good or bad, is not particularly important to the actual mechanism of teaching the ABC's or the times tables. But it is vital in the transmission of pride and respect. And, you know, not only does an attractive, well-groomed appearance help him impart these qualities to his students, but it also makes him feel good in the process.

Fortunately not all slobs in the classroom are slob-slobs. From this extreme they exist in all degrees of slobism down to mini-slobs. Most of us, at times, are afflicted with a touch of mini-slobism. Why put on a tie when an open collar will do? Why wear a jacket when a sport shirt will get by? And for the ladies, why a dress and nylons when slacks are far less bother? Or, "I won't fix my hair today. No one will notice this once." It's not easy to immunize oneself against slobism. The disease is highly contagious, and the germs are everywhere.

At this point I can't resist a minor digression. Several years ago my family and I spent a delightful six months in Holland where I was working on an engineering assignment. The Dutch in particular, and I guess Europeans in general, are the epitome in anti-slobism. A Dutchman, I am certain, would be just as embarrassed to be seen in public without a coat and tie as without his trousers. Many times I have witnessed a Dutchman in a suit and tie sitting in the grass along the bank of a canal, fishing pole in hand, tackle box at his side. One day at the plant where I was working I even saw a man, a foreman I assume, spreading asphalt on a driveway. You guessed it. In a suit and tie.

Somewhere along the line most of us Americans seem to have lost this part of our European heritage. I am not suggesting that we should regain all of it. But a little now and then wouldn't hurt. Our teachers claim to be professionals. And they should be. Let them look the part.

THE DEPARTURE FROM DISCIPLINE

Another heritage long since forgotten in many circles is our faith in discipline. Our Puritan ancestors are well remembered as strong exponents of the "spare the rod and spoil the child" theory. But alas, today, their contemporary "progressive" descendants have all but forgotten this sage advice. The Dr. Spock disciples have taken over. And with them a frightening toll in maladjusted lives. Even the good doctor himself, I am told, is now backpeddling a bit and is advocating stronger discipline.

You have heard the arguments, I am sure. Never discipline a child. Never speak to him harshly. It might inhibit him — destroy his creativity. If he pounds a nail into your Victorian coffee table, smile sweetly and reason with him. If he uses your best sofa for a trampoline simply supply him with pillows so that if he falls off he doesn't break his spoiled little neck.

Above all, never say "NO." He is only young once. Give him everything he wants. Mother, go to work if necessary, even if it means leaving him alone after school. Suppose you *can't* help him with his homework. Aren't you working your fingers to the bone in order to give him "everything?"

Pitiful, isn't it. And the most surprising thing of all is that those who subscribe the most strongly to this doctrine are not the "ignorant" masses but the so-called "educated" intellectuals.

For many years our schools resisted this wave of permissiveness. The stern schoolmarm, complete with hickory stick, was not about to buy such drivel. But gradually she too was forced to give in, or, as often was the case, simply gave up and was replaced by a sweet young product of one of our progressive teachers' colleges.

And then the trouble *really* began. Permissiveness in the home was bad enough, but in the school it was a disaster. Let the child proceed at his own pace was the cry. Don't hurry him. When he's ready, he will learn to read. When he feels like learning his arithmetic, he will do so. Don't teach him to stay within the lines when he is crayoning. Let him be expressive. And above all, don't discipline him. If he persists in running around the classroom, by all means permit him to do so. If he doesn't want to recite his multiplication tables today, wait until tomorrow. Be flexible. Adjust your schedule to suit his, never the reverse. Never regiment him. Don't arrange the chairs in your room in orderly, straight rows, don't line up your children and march them to the playground for recess. Let them run. They are *individuals,* not *robots.*

Make every effort to relate to your students. Get down to their level. Don't set yourself up on a pedestal. Insist that they call you by your first name, never "Miss Jones." This will make them regard you as a "pal," as an equal.

Corporal punishment? Not on your life. The paddle is as old-fashioned and ineffective as the horse and buggy. Only those with warped, sadistic minds would even consider using a paddle on a child.

Hogwash! The kindest and most valuable service a parent or a teacher can perform for a child is to administer firm, impartial discipline — including paddling if necessary. And sometimes it *is* necessary. *Conversely, the cruelest thing we can do to a child is to fail to discipline him.*

Someone has said that if God had believed in today's permissiveness He would have given us not the ten commandments, but the ten *suggestions!*

When I speak of discipline, incidentally, I mean discipline in its broadest sense, not just behavioral discipline. The child must indeed be taught how to behave and how to follow rules. He must be made to understand that rules are designed to benefit the majority, and that if he violates the rules he will be punished. Ideally he gets this training at home. But if the home fails, the school must take over. Otherwise the end result can be only chaos and anarchy. We in the schools cannot simply use the lack of training in the home as an excuse to do nothing. All too often, I am afraid, this has been done.

In addition to behavioral discipline, the child must also be taught to discipline his mind. How to develop good work and study habits. How to set priorities. How to be responsible. How to get his work done when it is due. How to be neat and orderly. How to be punctual. Pardon me if I blush a bit at this point. Many of us adults, I fear, need to take a refresher course in some of the areas.

Are our schools teaching discipline? If I am to judge from my personal observations in our own district plus the many many letters I receive from other districts, the answer is a resounding *"no."* Oh I don't mean that children are completely uncontrolled in most classrooms although all too often I've seen precisely just that. But for the most part there isn't much real, old-fashioned discipline either.

There are some exceptions. Recently I walked unannounced into an elementary school classroom — not in our Fundamental School, by the way — and was astonished to see the young, attractive, Black teacher with a yardstick in her hand. Almost apologetically and with some embarrassment she said to me, "I just seem to be able to maintain better control holding on to this thing." The children, by the way, as anyone could see after only a few minutes in that classroom, were deeply in love with their teacher. And it was equally obvious that real learning was taking place.

Isn't it sad that the teacher felt a bit guilty about using discipline? Our "progressive" teachers' colleges have left their mark on the minds of their graduates. Fortunately this lovely lady escaped with only a slight guilt complex. She must have had a crackerjack master teacher for her practice teaching to undo the brainwashing. Thousands of other young teachers, unfortunately, are not so lucky. Neither are their students.

THE ABSENCE OF ATTRACTIVENESS

One of the major problems in our schools today, especially our secondary schools, is that for many of their students they have absolutely no attraction. These same students, because of their complete lack of interest, assume the role of inmates, and behave accordingly. Many of our states now have laws that require complusory attendance until age eighteen, but as most schools are now constituted this is a mixed blessing. The old adage, "You can lead a horse to water, but you can't make him drink," was never more applicable. We force a child to go to school, shove him into a class in which he has absolutely no interest, and then wonder why he not only fails to learn anything, but is disruptive in the process.

Truancy has reached epidemic porportions. Absenteeism at our Pasadena high schools on any normal day commonly runs ten percent, often much higher. Police officers tell us that juveniles under eighteen, very often truants from school, are responsible for most daylight burglaries, assaults, and muggings. Ironic, isn't it? We force a child to go to school, thereby keeping him from getting a job and earning some money legitimately, so he plays hookey and picks up the cash he wants by snatching ladies' purses or breaking into homes.

All this business of forcing the child to stay in school might make some sense if our schools were really teaching the child something useful. Unfortunately in most instances they are not. Let's take a look at the typical "hard-core" truant. First of all he is achieving at least two or three years below grade level. He, by the way, is just as likely to be a "she," and he exists in all colors and in all socioeconomic levels. He is not involved in either varsity or intramural athletics. Nor does he play in the band or the orchestra, or belong to the drill team. For him school is a drag. He has absolutely no interest in being there. He could care less if he flunks every course on his schedule, and normally he does — or *would* if his teachers were not instilled with the philosophy of never failing a child. He is disruptive to the class. Always sits in the back of the room. Rarely participates in any discussion, and never does any homework. Suspension or explusion carry absolutely no threat to him, since he doesn't want to be in school in the first place. Except possibly as a convenient meeting place to visit with his friends, school for him has no attraction.

The athlete, on the other hand, has a real desire to be in school. He may or may not have any more actual academic interest than the hard-core truant, but he is well aware that if he falls too far behind in his studies or gets into too much trouble, he won't be able to play on the team. And, except for members of the opposite sex, playing on the team is just about the most attractive thing he can think of at the moment. To him, explusion or suspension is a real threat. Result. He behaves himself. He studies a bit — at least enough to stay on the team. And he learns something of value in the process. Rarely do our top-notch athletes in a well-run high school or junior high school get into serious trouble.

Not everyone, of course, can participate in athletics. Some are physically unable. Some simply are not interested. And herein lies the key. Somewhere, somehow, we must develop programs in our schools that are attractive to our young people. That will make them want to stay in school, not simply count the days until they can get out.

In no way am I suggesting that our schools should merely become instruments for play and entertainment. I do believe, however, that each child should be offered an occasional dish of ice cream along with his spinach and carrots. Call it bribery if you will, but wise parents have used the technique most effectively for centuries. Why not our schools? And remember, ice cream, too, is highly nutritious if it is consumed in moderation as a part of a well-balanced diet.

THE PAUCITY OF PATRIOTISM

Our guilt feelings about discipline are minuscule compared to the concerns that arise when we discuss patriotism. I must admit that even as I write this section, I wonder how I can make my point without being considered some sort of a flag-waving extremist. Why should this be? Why are we reluctant to talk about patriotism, much less teach it to our children?

I suppose the answer lies once again in the fact that we have been conditioned not to rock the boat. The moderate is universally painted as a good guy, not simply as an uninformed, wishy-washy individual who can't make up his mind and therefore chooses the middle of the road. Someone has said, by the way, that only two things belong in the middle of the road: a yellow stripe and a dead skunk. On the other hand, those with strong convictions, either to the right or to the left, are automatically dubbed as extremists. And to be called an extremist these days seems by many to be a fate feared worse than death.

So it is with patriotism. How many teachers today would dare suggest a patriotic assembly program? A real wing-ding. Patriotic speeches. Songs. Flag waving. The whole bit. Precious few! Especially at the high school level. Why? Because we have somehow become conditioned to believe that there is something wrong, something corny if you will, about such displays of emotion.

Remember the old parades and how the tingles went up and down your spine as the colors passed in revue and the band broke into the first few bars of "It's a Grand Old Flag?" Felt might good, didn't it? And somehow I can't believe it can be all that sinful. "Mass hysteria," you say. Of course. But why not? Far better than the completely passive, unemotional, and sometimes downright subversive attitudes in our schools today.

I am still shocked — although I've grown accustomed to it — to see how many students at our school board meetings refuse to salute the flag during our opening exercises. Their teachers still haven't quite mustered enough nerve to show such open defiance, although in most cases it is these very same teachers who have conditioned this behavior in their students. Sometimes, however, the students themselves recognize that something is wrong.

Two recent editorials in two different high-school newspapers bring out this point. In one the writer complained that at a sporting event two well-placed school administrators failed to stand at attention during the playing of the national anthem, and in fact talked to each other constantly during the entire rendition.

The second editorial was even more incriminating. Let me quote it in its entirety, omitting only the name of the high school and the name of the writer.

THE AMERICAN FLAG: SCAPEGOAT OR SYMBOL

The American flag. Does it mean anything today? If what — High School students think of the flag salute is any indication, I think not.

My understanding of the school district policy is that students are supposedly given the opportunity to say the pledge of allegiance, but are not required to do so. On the third day of school, my first period teacher gave the class the opportunity to stand and say the pledge of allegiance. The teacher had made some comments earlier about the possibility of the absolescence of the flag salute today. These comments motivated me to stay in my seat and observe, in order to see if any students would rise and pledge their allegiance to the flag.

Surprisingly, or maybe not so surprisingly, not a single student rose to salute the flag.

Some students object to the flag salute because they feel it is wrong to pledge allegiance to a symbol. Others may have lost faith in American government during the Watergate affair. Most charitably, some students may be afraid to stand up in front of the class and say the pledge of allegiance because they feel it is 'out;' that patriotism is not the thing to have. The most frightening thought is perhaps there is just a large underlying level of apathy prevalent in America today.

Although no students said the salute, the teacher did go through the motions pledging his allegiance to the flag. However, his pledge was modified slightly from the traditional, 'with liberty and justice for all.' His version went: 'with freedom and justice for all, almost.' While there is certainly not liberty and justice for all in the United States, this is an ideal towards which we can strive. While everyone is entitled to his own opinion, I don't particularly feel that a teacher should be modifying the pledge of allegiance. The pledge of allegiance, though not perfect, typifies an America of which we can all look forward to and work towards.

This of course, is only one particular teacher in one high school. Hopefully, I would be exaggerating if I said it was typical of most high schools across the country. But I would be equally inaccurate if I shrugged it off as merely an isolated instance.

Ironically enough, when I talked to him, the student who wrote the editorial defended his teacher. He was most disturbed at the reaction his statements had precipitated. The teacher, also, spoke up loudly in defense of his actions and the teachers' unions joined in the outcry. "How dare you question the behavior of this dedicated teacher?" "The very idea!" "He hasn't done anything wrong." "He can't help it if his students don't want to salute the flag."

I strongly disagree. As the teacher introduced the subject of saluting the flag, think what a few positive, patriotic statements would have done for that class. Suppose he said something like this:

Good morning, everyone. Each day at this time I will lead the class in the pledge of allegiance to the flag of our country. You are not required to join me if your personal or religious beliefs convince you that you should do otherwise. Nor should you feel embarrassed. Please, however, as a courtesy to me and to the other members of the class, stand quietly during the ceremony. I am well aware that all is not perfect in the United States. My generation has made some mistakes. It has also produced some fantastic accomplishments, including victory over polio and landing a man on the moon. Your generation should be proud of its heritage, proud to be a part of this great nation. This does not mean that you should condone things that you believe are wrong. Quite the contrary; you should strive with every ounce of your strength to correct them, being ever so careful, however, in the process, not to destroy the things that are good.

The flag is the symbol of our country. To salute it means simply that every time you do so you reaffirm your belief in the principles *for which it stands. And that you will defend those principles against all who would destroy them. Liberty and justice for all. Perhaps my generation has **not** yet fully reached this goal. But what a challenge for your generation to try to attain. Now, those of you who wish to do so, rise and join me in the pledge of allegiance.*

What sort of response do you suppose this same teacher would have received from this same class if he had made such a speech? I'll wager that better than 95 percent of his students would have jumped to attention and participated in a *meaningful* pledge — not simply parroted the words.

Patriotism is a precious commodity. Children do not learn it automatically. It must be taught. Teaching it properly is not easy. In fact it may require more expertise than teaching a child to read. Far too few teachers I fear, have tried to develop this expertise.

THE CONDEMNATION OF COMPETITION

Of the myriad problems our public schools face today, none is more serious than the lack of competition. In fact most of the other problems would simply fade away if we were somehow able to put competition back into our schools as well as into our lives.

Unfortunately, *competition,* like *discipline* and *patriotism,* has become a dirty word. Somehow we have been conditioned to consider it immoral, or, at the very least, unethical. Only in sporting events, it seems, do we still consider it honorable to be a winner. In all other areas of our lives we meekly accept the pablum that all should get an equal share. No one should win. No one should lose. Winner take all? How horrible.

And right here is the crux of the problem. Nearly every major accomplishment in the history of the world has been brought about by honest, free enterprise competition. Conversely, as soon as competition is eliminated, deterioration and inefficiency are inevitable.

The postal service is the classic example, although there are hundreds of others. Today in 1976 it costs 13 cents to mail a one-ounce letter across town. And we are told that the operation loses money constantly. I won't even talk about the efficiency or the reliability of this competition-free monopoly. At the same time, by means of privately operated shipping companies, competing against each other for business, and making a profit in the process, a gallon of crude oil or gasoline can be transported half way around the world for about three-and-one-half cents.

Our public school system suffers from precisely the same lack of competition as the postal service. In most communities, parents have absolutely no choice of where they may send their children to public school. Nor do they have any real yardstick to tell how good a job a particular school is doing in relation to another school — until it is too late. Most districts would never think of releasing test scores on an individual school basis. And in fact most overall district scores are so clouded with double talk when they *are* published that parents have no idea whether the

18

statistics are good or bad. Even the state-wide test scores are contrived in such a manner that it is impossible to compare them with scores from another state. Why? Quite simple. To avoid competition.

Even if mother or father is convinced that Johnny isn't learning as much as he should, what can be done about it? Precious little. Oh yes, of course, mother can and should attend the parent-teacher conferences. Usually this results in soothing, well-rehearsed and well-used phrases like, "Johnny just isn't quite ready. One of these days, he'll catch on like wildfire." And even if mother doesn't buy all this sweet talk, even if she convinces the principal that the teacher is doing a lousy job, what can the principal do? Again, very little.

Actually this is not entirely true. The really dedicated principal who is not afraid to rock the boat when necessary may possibly succeed in shoving the incompetent teacher off onto someone else. Or she may, with constant counseling, even be able to improve the teacher's performance a bit. But fire her? Never! Tenure, you know.

In fact, and most people do not realize this, it is just about as difficult to dismiss a first year probationary teacher as it is to remove a tenured teacher. Even with declining enrollments, the teachers' unions make staff reductions almost impossible, and then insist on cutting down strictly on the basis of seniority — not on merit.

Someone has said, not without a great deal of validity, that incompetent teachers are never fired. They simply are promoted to administrators.

Our private schools, especially the non-parochial ones, quite unlike our public schools, are strongly controlled by the rules of free enterprise competition. Either they turn out a good product, or they go out of business. It's as simple as that.

Recently some noteworthy attempts have been made to introduce competition into the public schools. The so-called voucher system is one example. Our Fundamental School in Pasadena is another.

Whatever the method, significant advances in the quality of our public educational system will most certainly be made, if it is somehow injected with a liberal dosage of life-preserving competition.

II
THE CAUSES

And so we have identified at least some of the problems that are widespread in our schools today. Problems that have developed. Problems that at one time in our history either were far less severe or did not exist at all. What has caused them to develop?

In any area as complex as education, no single cause could possibly be identified as the chief culprit. Instead there are a myriad of reasons for the current dilemma. None of them simple. Many of them interrelated. For lack of a better grouping, let's start at the top of the organizational structure and work down.

THE BOARDS OF EDUCATION

Most public school districts in the United States are designed so that in theory at least they are managed by elected boards of education. Usually board members serve either without pay or for a very minimal compensation. The elections are non-partisan.

To be a member of the board of education was once considered quite an honor. An honor reserved only for the most distinguished citizens of the community. Remember how the students and teachers alike literally quaked in their boots when their classroom was visited by a member of the board of education? He was both feared and respected. It was he who decided whether the children of the community were being properly educated. It was he who selected and approved the textbooks and placed his blessing on the curriculum.

Usually if a citizen became highly revered enough to be elected to the board of education, he remained on the board for life. Oh, of course, the townspeople went through the motions of reelecting the board member every few years or so, but rarely were there any major shakeups. Stability was the rule, not the exception. Controversy? Almost unheard of. My, how times have changed!

Today, except possibly in some of our smaller, rural communities, school board members are highly controversial. Rarely do they remain in office for more than a few yuears — either because they are rejected by the voters or because they simply can't stand the fighting any longer. Pressure groups are constantly on their backs. Parents, PTA organizations, community task forces, bussing advocates, anti-bussing protestors, those who solicit more and more federal funds, those who despise federal funds, citizen groups who demand removal of objectionable textbooks, and others who insist on so-called freedom of speech and press, not to mention the most vocal group of all — the teachers' unions.

Board meetings are marathons, often lasting into the wee hours of the morning. For many, the name of the game is "Harass the Board." In most states all meetings must be open to the public. Often this means simply that decisions are based not on logical reasoning or as the result of careful study and consideration but simply on who has the largest cheering section in the audience.

Sometimes a new and particularly dedicated board member may resist, for a while at least, the boos and jeers of the cheering section, and choose to stand by his own convictions. Then the pressure groups resort to other tactics. The threatening letters and phone calls. The protest marches. The signs. The pickets. The strikes and work stoppages. And, of course, through it all, even though this vocal militant group may represent only a small segment of the community, the board member is constantly accused of being unresponsive to the wishes of the people, of not listening.

Unfortunately most responsible community members do not have the slightest idea that all of these things are going on. Rarely do they attend board meetings. They are busy caring for their families or earning a living. Or, alas, maybe watching television. When they *do* come to a board meeting, they are shocked. Sometimes they rally a few friends and resolve to become involved, but for the most part they shake their heads sadly and walk away.

The militants, on the other hand, never give up. If they lose a round or two, they simply retrench and return for the next round. Time is on their side, and they seem to have endless quantities of it at their disposal. I have seen them sit hour after hour at board meetings, waiting patiently through countless reports and statistics, simply hoping for the opportunity to pounce upon a weary board member in an unguarded moment. Eventually, of course, the moment comes, and the verbal abuse begins. Meeting after meeting. Hour after hour. The same faces. The same tactics. Time and time again.

Many of the protestors are teachers who, cloaked in the protective garb of tenure, feel perfectly free to level all manner of vindictive insults and intimidations at the board members who, in theory, are their bosses. When they are particularly aroused, they enlist the aid of their students who blindly latch onto their teachers' causes and join in the melee. After all, it's much more fun than doing their homework. And the teacher is probably far too busy trying to harass the board to worry about assigning or correcting homework, anyway.

Then, in the unlikely event that the board stands firm against all this frontal assault, the attackers go to the polls. Recall elections are common. Rarely are they successful. But even when they fail, they take a devastating toll in time, money, and effort. Sooner or later the harassed and frustrated board member decides that saving the school district simply isn't worth the strain on his own life and health and that of his family, and throws in the sponge. Voila! The militants have won again. Even though they may represent only a small fraction of a percent of the total population of the community.

Those of us who are students of history are well aware of the dozens of instances where small bands of dedicated revolutionaries, almost always less than ten percent of the citizenry, have completely seized control of entire nations by just such tactics. The methods are highly effective and extremely difficult to combat, especially when the honest, highly principled majority abides by all the rules of ethics and fair play and the militants have no such restrictions.

The net result? Only the most dedicated or the most foolish — or the militants themselves — are willing to serve on boards of education. Certainly no businessmen who depends upon the public to buy his wares or services can risk financial ruin to do so. And even the relatively independent citizen risks serious damage to his health and reputation.

This is, of course, tragic. If our civilization is to survive and prosper, it is absolutely essential that our educational system be governed by men and women of the highest qualifications. Persons who are well educated, and have broad experience. Persons who have been highly successful in their own lives. Persons who because of their actions and reputations are known to be of good character and of strong moral convictions.

Once again look at history. Rarely has a major civilization fallen as the result of a frontal attack by outside forces. Almost always demise has been brought about by internal decay and deterioration. Our boards of education may well be the most important groups of elected officials in our nation today. Their actions may have an infinitely greater influence on our destiny than those of apparently higher ranking officials, including congressmen, senators, and even presidents. An illiterate nation cannot long survive. Somehow we must once again return qualified, responsible citizens to our boards of education.

THE TEACHERS' UNION

All over America teachers' unions are gaining a stranglehold on school districts. The old slogan, "You can't have your cake and eat it too," may apply in some areas but teachers are clearly exempt. Not only do they enjoy the far-reaching benefits and protections of civil service as well as the almost impenetrable cloak of tenure, but they are rapidly acquiring the paralyzing capability of the unions, including the right of collective bargaining and the right to strike.

Civil service regulations were designed to afford fair working conditions, practices, and salaries to those who by law were denied the right to strike. It was reasoned, quite logically, that strikes, stoppage and slowdowns are unthinkable among civil service employees. Therefore special protection and benefits were built into civil service contracts. Now, however, teachers have both the protection of civil service and the power of the unions at their disposal. Against such a double-barreled threat, school boards, parents, and taxpayers are virtually helpless.

In a recent statewide election beginning with the governor's race, the California Teachers' Association openly donated $327,000 to candidates who espoused their views, particularly with respect to collective bargaining. In my own community of Pasadena, the militant teachers' unions initiated a recall against my colleagues and me, and donated $10,000 in money and thousands of hours in time in an unsuccessful effort to unseat us from the board of education.

As I am writing this manuscript, I was informed by our superintendent that a grievance has just been filed by the union because a history teacher was directed by her principal to teach a ninth grade class next semester instead of the twelfth grade she prefers. This particular teacher, I am informed, had never taught high school before last term, and although she had done a creditable job in junior high, she was not performing well, in the principal's judgment, with the older children. Therefore the reassignment. The union contends that the principal has no right to make this change, and our attorneys tell us that decisions on similar cases in the past have frequently sided with the union. A sad commentary!

California state law requires that teachers be notified by April 1 if their services may not be needed the following school year. Because most school systems these days are faced with declining enrollment the April notices are becoming increasingly common. The unions contend that they, not the boards of education, have the right to dismiss teachers. In our own district, teachers staged a most disruptive, one-day strike because we mailed these dismissal notices to our first and second year probationary teachers.

Several years ago in a nearby district the board was sued by the union because two of the 43 probationary teachers that were given notices were actually terminated. After a long and costly court battle, one teacher was ordered reinstated with full back pay and given tenure. The other who had left the district was granted approximately twice the amount of back pay he would have earned. The union newsletter, in gloating over the victory, stated that the fact that there were no mass layoffs of teachers the following year showed that the district had "learned a lesson," since the proceedings had cost the district more money than it would have cost to reemploy the two teachers in the first place. In that same newsletter, the union proudly boasted that through a series of lawsuits in a labor dispute they had brought another school board to its knees.

During our salary negotiations last year, our board of education granted the teachers a blanket across-the-board raise of six-and-a-half percent. In addition we set aside two-and-a-half percent in a special fund to be distributed to individual school personnel and teachers based on a performance evaluation. We called the program a Performance Incentive Plan. Evaluations were based on such things as test scores, absenteeism, vandalism, appearance of the campus, parent satisfaction, and so on. In this way, we reasoned, some good healthy competition could be set up among our various schools. Our better teachers and staff would be rewarded with a bonus, and our poorer ones would be encouraged to improve their ways or look elsewhere for employment.

All year long the unions fought our incentive plan. It was even one of the reasons given as the basis for staging the recall election. When the recall failed, the unions went to the courts and filed an injunction against us. Currently we are prohibited from further work on the plan until the court decides whether we, the elected representatives of the people, have the *right* to institute such a program. The unions claim we do not, and demand that we divide the incentive-fund money equally among all the teachers.

Unfortunately this power struggle is nationwide. Public education is the largest business in the world. Its control is rapidly being wrested from the hands of the elected representatives of the people who pay for it, by a huge monolithic labor organization called the National Education Association. It has been said that in just a few years no person will be able to be elected to public office, including that of the President of the United States, without the approval of the NEA.

TENURE

Whenever an artificial restraint is placed upon a natural law, such as the law of supply and demand, inefficiency invariably results. Tenure is a perfect example.

In theory, tenure was designed to protect good, experienced teachers from the whims of supposedly insensitive or vindictive administrators, or even the economy-minded, axe-wielding school boards. In some cases it presumably serves this purpose. Unfortunately, no one has yet enacted an effective law to protect the student, the parent, and the taxpayer from the havoc caused by tenure.

Truly excellent teachers just like top-notch scientists, engineers, craftsmen, businessmen, attorneys, or any other group of workers, need no artificial protection. Except possibly during brief periods of economic depression or unusual circumstance, the natural law of supply and demand assures adequate, well-compensated employment for these highly sought individuals. Tenure, therefore, does absolutely nothing for the good teachers. Indeed it harms them by protecting the mediocre and poor teachers. And far worse, it drives at least one very large and significant nail into the coffin of our public education system.

Just as a forest needs to be cleared of its deadwood if it is to remain healthy, so must the ranks of teachers be thinned periodically if we are to maintain top quality in our schools. This is not nearly so heartless as it sounds. All successful business organizations use the system most effectively. Without it they simply could not survive. In actual practice only the worst misfits are usually discharged and they invariably find positions in other areas where they are far happier and infinitely more effective. In fact, dissatisfaction or unsuitability is probably why they were doing a poor job in the first place. Discharging them may be the biggest favor anyone ever did for them.

For those remaining in the organization, the very knowledge that they *can* be fired is a most effective deterrent against slovenliness and mediocrity. Just imagine how efficient a business would be if all of its employees knew that regardless of how poorly they worked they could not be laid off. But then why imagine? The largest single business in the nation today, our public school system, operates on precisely this principle.

The situation is even worse than most people realize. In most states it is just about as difficult to release a first year "probationary" teacher as it is to remove a tenured teacher. In California there is almost no difference. And unless the probationary teacher is very nearly incompetent, with reams of backup evidence and evaluations to prove his incompetency, he must be laid off strictly on a seniority basis. Therefore, if a school district is forced to cut down on its staff because of declining enrollment — and this itself is made extremely difficult by legal roadblocks — it has absolutely no choice of which teachers it may let go.

For all too many years the parents and taxpayers of this nation have sat by idly while the education lobbyists have instituted laws to protect themselves. We and our children are now reaping the "benefits" of that legislation.

FAILURE

Failure, like firing, was once used to inform individuals that their performance was unsatisfactory. Unfortunately, in the eyes of our modern educators, failure has become a definite no-no. "Think of the irreparable harm to the child," they say, "if he is held back a year. Think what it means to him if he is not permitted to continue with his class." Rubbish! Of course there are some psychological effects, but the child soon adjusts, finds new friends, and maybe even is able to keep himself near the head of his new class instead of way, way behind. His entire outlook may change. When the teacher asks him a question, he knows the answer. In fact for the first time he realizes that he is smarter than some of his classmates, and he far prefers this new role to that of the class imbecile.

Conversely, what happens if the child is passed on year after year? Oh yes, he keeps his same friends and classmates, but he also keeps his same image. And always, each year, he gets further and further behind. Never, except in extremely unusual circumstances, does he ever catch up. And unfortunately, this lag behind his peers does not disappear when his school days are over. It follows him like a dark ominous shadow through his entire life.

Not only does this "prohibition against failure" policy hurt the child who should have been held back, but it also severely restricts the learning potential of the rest of the class. I mentioned earlier how at one Pasadena junior high school, 25 eighth graders scored at the fourth grade level or lower in their achievement tests. And I am sure that Pasadena is no isolated case.

So the problem is not simply that one or two slow students should have been held back. Possibly at the elementary grades this might be the case. Indeed this is why any necessary retention *should* be done early in the child's school career if at all possible. When it is not done, by the time the higher grades are reached, the error compounds itself until a significant portion of the class is way below grade level. And that below-level group inevitably brings down the achievement level of the rest of the class. Is it any wonder that in schools all over America test scores are plummeting?

Unfortunately, once the crime of passing a child on to the next grade regardless of his achievement is begun, it is never remedied. At the end of each succeeding year the teacher is only too glad to shove the victim along with his classmates. Heaven forbid that she should be stuck with him for another year! After all, wasn't he foisted onto her by his former teacher? And so, on and on, year after year, until the time arrives for graduation. "Aha," you say. "Now comes the day of reckoning. The poor child will not be able to meet his graduation requirements, and, therefore, will not get his diploma."

Sadly, you are wrong. The game of make-believe continues. Without even a crossed finger or a tongue in cheek, and with the strains of "Pomp and Circumstance" floating through the air, the principal solemnly reads the victim's name, hands him his diploma, shakes his hand, and sends him on his way — either to college, or to make his living in the cold, cruel world.

If he goes to college, the masquerade often continues, because many of our colleges today either subscribe to the "no failure" theory or have lowered their standards. In order not to make you feel too uneasy, I won't carry our sub-standard graduate on to medical school or beyond. But let me say simply that sooner or later one of two things happens. Either he finds that he is not equipped to compete with his peers in a free society or society lowers itself to his level of proficiency. If he does not go on to college, precisely the same thing happens, only sooner. His employer does not reward him for effort or attendance — only results. If he cannot produce, he is discharged.

Some of you may have read the story about a young man from San Francisco who was discharged from the Air Force after only one month's service because he was unable to read. His mother was horrified. "How on earth did he graduate from high school if he can't read?" she asked. Then she made some caustic comments about our school system. "Why are our schools doing this to the children today? A cap of knowledge on their heads, and they can't even spell Mississippi." Then she reflected that she had never gotten past the sixth grade but that she had been held back for two years in the fifth grade because she couldn't spell *mischief.* "You know," she said, "I only had a sixth grade education, but I can write a business letter and make out a money order. If my son can only read at the third grade level, how's he going to find a job?"

The high school authorities were not the least bit surprised. They stated that diplomas are a matter of course. The student has only to fulfill a certain number of hours to qualify for graduation.

California State Senator H.L. Richardson, a long-time member of the Senate Committee on Education, wrote a special report discussing the plight of this young man. He concluded by saying:

Educating the young is secondary. The primary function is to get them in, collect the ADA (Average Daily Attendance) and ship them out. Each student must average so many days a year in school so that the school district can collect state aid. In other words, each student represents so much on the hoof to the school district.

For example, if a student is dropped from school because of poor grades, then the dollars that he represents would be cut off. If this happened to enough students, a teacher might not be needed and that would be horrible. If a few teachers were dismissed, then an administrator might have to go. Heaven forbid! If that were the case, the California Teachers Association would not get their dues and their lobbyists in Sacramento might not get paid as much.

Maybe, just maybe, these reasons should be considered when we review why this young man was kept in high school and then graduated. Maybe the fact that he can't get a job isn't that important to the educational bureaucrats. Their only concern might be keeping jobs for their colleagues in the educational establishment and the children be damned.

ABILITY GROUPING

Another "old-fashioned" idea that has come into disrepute among modern educators is that children should be grouped in the classroom according to their ability. In the one-room schoolhouse, grouping was not possible, but as consolidation took place and schools became larger most administrators divided the children at each elementary grade level into classes according to ability. The slow learners in one class. Average students in another. Accelerated children in a third. There was, of course, some overlapping, but for the most part each class was relatively homogeneous.

At the secondary level the schools normally were larger, thereby permitting an even more sophisticated grouping. At one high school with which I am familiar, there were eight separate tracks in the so-called tracking system.

Today, however, the tracking system has been discontinued at that high school as well as at the elementary schools feeding it. You have heard the arguments, I am sure. It is very damaging, we are told, to place children in niches. Think how it will inhibit them to know they are in the "dumbell" class. And besides, none of the teachers wants to teach such a class. Finally we are told — and I have been given this line ad nauseum — that mixing the good students with the poor students in the classroom inspires the poor students to greater heights, and has absolutely no effect upon the good students. This same rub-off or osmosis theory is expounded by the busing advocates who claim they can raise the test scores of minority children simply by placing them in the same classroom with higher achieving children.

Does it work? Of course not. And in Pasadena we have years of sad experience and reams of data to prove it. Instead of raising the test scores of the poor students, the scores of *all* the students are brought down, and brought down precipitously. Why? Quite simple.

First of all, the good student rapidly learns that he has a lead-pipe cinch. He sees that very little effort is required to keep up with the mean level of the class, and he applies himself accordingly — with very little effort. Furthermore, he rapidly becomes bored and disinterested. And instead of *helping* the poorer student, he is far more likely to look upon him with disdain and ridicule.

Conversely, the low achiever sees very quickly that he cannot keep up with the rest of the class, and soon gives up trying. Although he resents it, he adjusts to feeling inferior because he is constantly reminded that he cannot compete with the better students. Inborn within him, however, there still lies that competitive spark that is a vital part of most of us. Since he is unable to compete academically, he competes physically, often by disrupting the class to gain attention. He becomes either the class clown or the class bully, whichever better suits his personality. In either event, the net result is not only absence of learning but utter chaos.

The teacher is caught smack in the middle of an impossible situation. If she tries to concentrate on the poor student, the quality level of the class drops off and the better students are bored. Likewise if she gears her lesson to the top of the class, the bottom group is completely at sea — and usually writhing and churning to boot. So she tries to teach at some median level and both ends suffer.

There is never such a thing as a completely homogeneous classroom, nor would such a situation necessarily be desirable. In any class, there is always a graduation of abilities. The better students. The average students. The below average. But for effective learning to take place the spread among these three groups must be kept within reasonable limits. In many of our schools I strongly suspect these limits have far exceeded all reasonable bounds, and classroom performance has declined accordingly. This same effect, incidentally, is the chief reason why forced busing for ethnic balance has been a disaster wherever it has been tried. Pasadena is a perfect example.

It has long been recognized that minority children's test scores, in general, fall well below those of Anglo-Caucasian children at the same age level. This is why busing was proposed in the first place, to bring up the achievement level of minority children. Certainly a laudable and most necessary objective.

When children enter first grade in Pasadena they are given readiness tests. Interestingly, our Black children score nearly as well on these tests as the white children do, about eleven points above the national norm. By the time they reach fifth grade, however, the Black children have fallen two full years behind their white counterparts on the achievement tests. By twelfth grade, they are four years behind! This is in completely integrated, ethnically-balanced classrooms. Spanish surname children test slightly higher than the Black children, but still considerably below the Anglos.

The phenomenon is very real. It is not imagined. Visualize a teacher trying to teach a class where there is a two, three, or four year spread among the students. A group of seventh graders, for example, in the eleventh grade classroom. The fact that these low achievers are, for the most part, minorities, has absolutely no relevance, except possibly as an excuse to blame the resulting chaos on racism. Precisely the same chaos would result if the below level students were white. Is it any wonder that classroom grouping strictly on the basis of ethnic balance has resulted in massive deterioration of the quality of education whenever it has been tried?

Conversely, *education is indeed the key to meaningful integration.* If we can devise a means of bringing up minority achievement levels, and with a little common sense I think we can, integration will follow naturally. The average, clear thinking, white American today is perfectly willing to accept a member of a minority race as his equal, as his fellow worker, as his boss, if that person is qualified to do his job. But when minorities are shoved into jobs beyond their capabilities, strictly because they *are* minorities, friction and resentment occur.

Closing the achievement gap is essential. It must be done. But destroying ability grouping by mixing everyone together in one massive potpourri is not the way to do it. Not only does that fail to improve the poor student but it also harms the good student, and makes life miserable for the teacher in the process.

LEARNING STATIONS

With the demise of ability grouping, educators were forced to come up with some new "innovation" as a replacement. It soon became apparent even to the most avid advocates of the osmosis theory that learning doesn't just rub off no matter how hard or how often poor students are rubbed against good students. But would the innovators admit their mistake and go back to ability grouped classrooms? Never! "Think of the glorious sociological experience these children are undergoing by mixing with others of different backgrounds and interests. So they aren't learning to read or write or to add or subtract. Look at all these other experiences they are gaining to help them learn to understand each other and to live together."

But secretely, I think, in spite of claiming to believe all these canned phrases they espouse, the new breed of educators feels a bit guilty about the fact that their students aren't learning. Somewhere in the dim dark past they remember hearing that the purpose of our schools is to educate. And occasionally their consciences tingle just a tiny bit. So they have come up with learning stations.

Learning stations are claimed to cure all the ills of the classroom. Primarily, however, they were designed to serve as a substitute for ability grouping. For the uninformed, each class is divided into small groups of five or six students, called learning stations. Instead of teaching the entire class, the teacher works with one station at a time while the other groups are on their own. Periodically, every half hour or so, the children pack up their belongings and shift to another station. In some schools this is quite a ceremony, complete with chimes and bells. At the first chime the children stand. At the second chime, they move to their next station, and so on. Almost like the changing of the guard.

Normally this is done strictly within each classroom but occasionally a group of teachers who have been especially well indoctrinated with the "team teaching" approach get together and expand the concept so that several classes are involved. At one school where my daughter was practice-teaching, there were 15 learning stations in her third grade class. All day long, every eight minutes, the bell rang and the children moved to another station. "Just as I was beginning to get through to one one group," my daughter lamented, "the bell rang and they were shoved along to the next table."

Fortunately most schools do not use such a mass production approach. But even in the normal situation the learning station concept creates far more problems than it solves. I have visited scores of such classrooms and almost always the pattern is precisely the same, especially at the primary, K-3, grade level.

At the teacher station, where the teacher is working with her group, all is well. The children are usually paying attention and genuine learning appears to be taking place. But at the other tables it is another story. Visualize five or six squirming first or second graders around a table, completely on their own, supposedly studying together or working on some sort of "learning" project.

Obviously, in order to avoid complete chaos, the learning projects must be designed to hold the children's interest without adult supervision. Therefore they invariably take the form of fun and games rather than study. The games, of course, are designed to be educational. And incidentally, or maybe not so incidentally, the classroom toy and game business is now a multi-million dollar operation.

Math toys are without question the most abundant. There are games of all descriptions, from simple cards for "crazy eights," to complex spinner boards or dice operated contests. Checkers and dominoes are also quite popular. Then there are the blocks. Thousands of them. In all colors, shapes, and sizes. Triangles. Squares. Hexagons. Rods. Cubes. Short. Long. Large. Small. Free standing. Interlocking. A block or shape for every occasion. All are supposed to help the child visualize his numbers facts. It's not good enough today for Johnny to learn that two times two equals four. He must understand *why* it is so. Unfortunately he commonly ends up learning neither.

The math learning station is usually a most interesting spot to visit. Invariably the children have moved from the table to the floor and, making full use of their ample supply of "learning" materials, have created all sorts of innovative designs and structures. Houses. Roads. Railroad tracks. Vehicles of all descriptions. Always I ask them what they are doing and always I get the most interesting answers! Some of them shake up the principal a bit if he happens to be accompanying me on my tour. I still chuckle about one most imposing structure that three third grade boys were constructing between two desks. When I asked what they were doing, the boys looked at me in utter disbelief that anyone could ask such a stupid question. "We're building a bridge," was their reply.

Then there is the cut-and-paste station where the children are supposed to be developing their small muscles. And the crayons. Everywhere crayons. When I see the amount of crayoning going on in our primary grades I can only conclude that in a few years America will undoubtedly lead the world in crayoning. Of course our professional crayoners may be illiterate, but if we can convince the Olympic committee to include crayoning as a sport, we should be assured a clean sweep of gold medals. We will have to make certain, however, that all instructions to the contestants are oral, not written.

The puzzle station is always quite popular. Puzzles have come a long way since the old jigsaw variety, although this basic type is still probably the most abundant. In theory, matching the pieces of a well designed puzzle may have some educational value, although more-and-more as I question students I doubt how much of the intended lesson is actually being transmitted. Again, without adult supervision, the lesson usually deteriorates into play.

Even the stations that at first glance would appear to be productive are often deceiving. The audiovisual station is such an example. Invariably when I am touring classrooms the principal edges me toward the group of children clustered around the audiovisual equipment and proudly proclaims that the array of cassette tape recorders and headsets is "just like having another teacher in the room." I am supposed to be impressed, nod my head affirmatively, and quickly pass on to the next area. But being of an inquisitive nature, and possibly just a wee bit sadistic, I always insist on watching the group for a few minutes.

In theory, the children are supposed to be listening to the tape and following along word by word in the book, thereby learning to read. In practice, however, unless my visits have all been most atypical, rarely are more than one third of the children gaining anything from the lesson. Most of them, I find, are not following the text. Many of them do not have the book open to the right page. Several, I have observed, did not even have the right book! When I pointed this out, the principal immediately flustered a bit and then flurried about from child to child flipping pages to get the audio and the visual into sync, meanwhile apologizing that the teacher had not instructed her students properly.

Have we in our frantic search for innovation completely lost our common sense? Do we really expect six or eight lively, wiggling first or second graders to sit quietly around a table for 30 minutes, carefully following instructions from a tape recorder, dutifully obeying its every command, and soaking up knowledge in the process? Let's not blame the teacher for all the ills of the classroom. Let's not oversimplify by sagely observing that if we had all good teachers our children would learn. Unquestionably, a shortage of truly top notch personnel has plagued our schools for years, but a significant part of the problem lies with the system, not the teacher.

On the other hand, teachers are really a part of the system, and even some of the older more experienced ones who ought to know better often become addicted to it. Frequently they forget how to teach, and instead turn into glorified supply clerks, spending most of their day dispensing and collecting toys and games. All too often, I fear, they come to enjoy their new role and will defend it to the bitter end, even in the face of precipitously declining test scores.

For some teachers, and I hope they are few, learning stations and their associated educational toys have become little more than glorified babysitters. A means of keeping children occupied so they do not become disruptive. Let me cite what I consider a tragic example.

During a visit to a sixth grade classroom I spotted a nice-looking, clean, well dressed boy sitting all by himself at a desk in one corner of the room. The usual audiovisual equipment was on the desk. Cassette recorder. Book. Headsets. The whole outfit. I walked up to the boy and asked what he was doing. "Listening to the Colts game," he politely replied. Picking up a spare headset I listened to the tape and heard a most exciting, play by play description of a Colts football game. Opening the book on the desk I saw the same story, complete with pictures. Obviously the boy was supposed to be following along in the book as he listened. "Could you read me a bit of this?" I asked. "I'm sorry," he said apologetically, "I can't read." I tried coaxing. "Don't be afraid, I won't laugh at your mistakes. Just try a line or two and I'll help you along." "No," he said, "I'm sorry. I just can't even begin."

It was obvious that the boy was sincere. He could not read. And his "reading" lesson for the day wasn't helping him one iota to learn. But it was keeping him occupied and out of trouble. And the teacher didn't have him in her hair. It made me feel like tearing mine out by the roots.

Sometimes teachers reach out pretty far trying to provide variety in their learning stations. At the 15-station, combined third grade class I talked about earlier, one of the stations was called the "get to know each other station." The props were a complete assortment of hats, coats, ties, shoes, etc. Students were instructed to dress each other so that they could learn to get along with each other.

I am well aware that many of my "progressive" associates believe that learning to get along with each other is an important part of one's schooling. But couldn't they do it during recess or the noon hour? In their zeal to be innovative and to try all manner of wonderful new techniques and ideas, teachers fail to realize that each day contains only a fixed amount of time. For every minute spent on these humanistic sidelights, even though they may be of some value, the same number of minutes are lost from teaching the basics. Here a minute. There a minuute. Little by little the tail begins wagging the dog.

PHONICS

In 1955 Rudolph Flesch published his book *Why Johnny Can't Read.* In it he warned of the danger of abandoning the long established phonics method of teaching reading in favor of the look-see method. Unfortunately, Flesch's warnings were pooh-poohed by most educators, and especially by the giants in the publishing industry who never had it so good. Not only were they selling new texts on the look-see method and countless variations thereof but also the market for remedial materials was literally exploding.

The look-see epidemic was not limited to the United States. In 1970 a Canadian housewife, Mary Johnson, published the book *Programmed Illiteracy In Our Schools.* In it she reports the results of a monumental survey taken in Canada, England and the United States. The results are overwhelming. Whenever the look-see method of teaching reading was used, children scored poorly on standard reading and spelling tests. Conversely, in the few schools where reading was still taught by phonics, test scores were perfectly normal.

Mrs. Johnson supports Flesch's twenty-year-old warnings with dramatic proof. Thousands of spelling papers and countless hours of tape-recorded, oral reading. She also points out some interesting statistics that just might explain why one of the most insidious and most damaging hoaxes of all time, the look-see method of teaching reading, has been so widely promoted.

One major international publisher of educational materials distributed more than six million pamphlets, she says, free of charge to elementary teachers. The pamphlet ridicules the "mechanical sounding out of words" and defends the sight method. The author of the publication, Mrs. Johnson points out, had earned more than two million dollars in royalties from textbooks she had written about the sight method. Hardly an impartial critic! And if royalties alone amounted to two million dollars, think about the profit to the publisher. Could it be that the publisher was a bit more interested in making a profit than in teaching children to read?

Mortimer Smith, former executive director of the Council for Basic Education, commenting on *Programmed Illiteracy in Our Schools,* stated, "The public generally may recognize, in Mrs. Johnson's story, the age old pattern of the innocent citizen's struggle to get answers and action from a bureaucracy which seems to be immovably set on a predetermined course."

Just as the calf-length dresses of yesteryear were replaced by the miniskirt, and now, heaven forbid, are coming back into style, also prompted almost entirely by the profit motive, so is phonics again coming back into vogue and the sight method is going out. The "in" thing among educators is to tell parents that their children are being taught by phonics, although usually they imply that the sight method is used as a supplement. They would never admit that the sight method has been a complete disaster and should be thrown out completely.

Then there is the "party line" that all children don't learn in the same way. Don't you believe it! I have yet to be convinced that *any* child can learn to read better by memorizing word pictures and shapes than by pure, unadulterated phonics.

On one classroom visit I stopped by a couple of boys madly feeding cards into a machine. Being an engineer, I am especially intrigued by mechanical gadgets. I was fascinated. The cards were about the same size as standard computer cards. On each of them a word such as JUMP, HOUSE, RUN, or WALK was printed in bold letters. As the card passed through the machine, with the word in full view of the student, the machine would speak, jump, jump, jump, run, run, run. The students, too, were fascinated, and seemed to be trying to see how fast they could insert the cards, probably in the hope that the machine would become confused or maybe even stutter. But the machine was perfect. Never skipped a beat. Never misprounced a word.

After watching for several minutes, I picked up three of the cards from the top of the pile and asked the boys to read them to me. The first card read JUMP, but two of the boys in unison assured me with conviction that it said WALK. The next two words were read with somewhat less assurance but with no improvement in accuracy. Rudolph Flesch and Mary Johnson would not have been the least bit surprised.

One of the worst features of the modern methods of teaching reading is that parents are frequently discouraged from helping their children. Only the professional teacher, parents are told, understands the proper technique. The poor child will only be hopelessly confused if the parent tries to help him.

Unfortunately it is a biological law of nature that most parents of elementary school students are new at the game, and teachers and administrators can be extremely convincing. It is hard for a young inexperienced parent to stand up to a teacher or a principal with an impressive array of degrees and tell him that he is wrong. Even the most stout hearted usually wilt when the educator cites his vast years of experience in working with hundreds of children who have had exactly the same problem as Johnny. Invariably, the parents back down, decide not to interfere, and leave poor Johnny in the hands of the professionals.

My own experience with each of my four children fits precisely into this pattern, up to a point. Being a stubborn Pennsylvania Dutchman, I ignored the teachers. When my oldest child started having reading problems in grammar school, my wife bought a Hay-Wingo phonics book. Every evening my daughter was instated on the sofa beside me (my choice, not hers) and we drilled, A is for Apple, B is for Bear, O is for Ostrich. I almost lost my sanity over SAM SAT IN THE SUN and THE SUN IS GOOD FOR SAM. For a while nothing happened, but suddenly, almost overnight it seemed, she began to catch on, and the whole world opened up to her. She could read. Ironically at the second semester of the first grade the *teacher* proudly announced that our daughter was reading on the fifth grade level.

Precisely the same thing happened with our three subsequent children, in almost exactly the same sequence, except that with the twins one sat on either side of me on the sofa. That, by the way, was an experience that could only be survived while one still retains the inexhaustible endurance and infinite patience of youth. Poor old Sam, however, finally did indeed find his seat in the sun, although the pages of Hay-Wingo were nearly worn out in the process.

Many, many times as I think back over that experience I ask myself what would have happened to my children's scholastic records if my wife and I had not helped them with their studies. Is it possible that the chief reason why minority children fall so far behind is because they so often lack parental supervision and assistance? And the irony of the whole situation is that even though today most educators are bemoaning the lack of involvement, and often use that lack as an excuse for their own short-comings, only yesterday — and in many schools even today — they were discouraging that very involvement.

Without question the English language is complicated and fraught with exceptions to the rules. But for centuries people have learned to read it successfully by employing a basic phonetic approach. Only when we deviated from that approach did we get into trouble.

NEW MATH

Precisely the same thing has been happening in the teaching of mathematics as in reading, and for precisely the same reasons. The "new math" promoted by the best PR men the textbook publishers could muster, has swept the nation like wildfire. Fortunately the main flame front seems to have passed and is now dying out, but a few residual hot spots still remain and need desperately to be mopped up.

Why Johnny Can't Add, by Morris Kline, is a Johnny-come-lately when compared to Rudolph Flesch's *Why Johnny Can't Read,* but it tells the same tragic story. Kline, a New York University mathematician says quite bluntly that the modern math movement was doomed to fail, first because of the incompetence of the curriculum writing team, but even more significantly because of the self-destructing warfare among the various projects that were competing for federal and foundation grants and textbook royalties. "The new-math people," he says, "instead of first testing their wares under closely controlled conditions, literally flooded the market with materials of unproven worth." Once again it would appear that the profit motive, rather than some revolutionary educational breakthrough provided the impetus for yet another assault against the minds of our children.

My objection to new math is not so much that it is inherently damaging, but simply that it wastes precious time. Instead of learning his multiplication tables, for example, the child spends hours studying set theory. Now I cannot honestly find anything harmful about set theory, but try as I will — and as a practicing engineer I am far more of a mathematician than most educators — for the life of me I can't find anything useful about it either.

There may be just a wee bit more justification for teaching various number bases, but not much. It is true that computers operate in Base 2 but humans all over the world count in Base 10. The student who learns his number facts in Base 10 can make change, balance a checkbook, compute sales tax, figure percentages, and perform all sorts of useful and necessary every day arithmetic exercises. If he should some day become involved with computer logic, a very short briefing will enable him to adjust to that language with very little effort. Conversely, if in his favorite years he wastes time studying abstract concepts that he will in all probability never need, and fails to learn the basics, he simply never catches up.

It's not that new math theory is particularly difficult. It isn't. Most children grasp it rather easily. But to do so takes time. Valuable time. Most of our younger generation have mastered its concepts with reasonable competence. Presumably they have gained a better understanding of how number systems function, and have acquired an appreciation for the beauty and the science of mathematics. But unfortunately all too many of these budding "new mathematicians" cannot add, subtract, multiply, or divide.

For the most part, the new math infestation has been limited to the primary and elementary grade levels. Here, because both parents and educators agree that it has been a disaster, it is slowly being exterminated. Not, however, without horrendous toll. But the innovators are always busy. Recently our board of education was asked to approve a federally funded pilot course in "new geometry." Oh, indeed it wasn't called new geometry. In fact when I asked the author whether his proposed program was to geometry what new math was to mathematics, he turned six shades of purple and refused to answer my question. An analysis of the course material, however, showed that this was precisely the case. Instead of learning the conventional geometric theorems, corollaries and proofs, the student would study the more abstract reasoning that led to the development of these basic laws. Sound familiar? Yes, the innovators are always busy.

NEW GRAMMAR

Have you looked at a grammar book lately? If it has been published in the last ten years or so, chances are you won't recognize it. Parts of speech? Nouns. Verbs. Adjectives. Adverbs. Prepositions. Participles. Infinitives. What in the world are they? Sentence diagramming. Subject. Direct object. Indirect object. Phrase. Clause. Never heard of them. Must be some sort of extinct or at least endangered species.

Some time ago a group of senior high students came before our board of education to protest taking the standard achievement tests. "The tests," they said, "are not meaningful and should be changed." One specific complaint was that the tests ask questions about grammar, "And we haven't been taught grammar for years." After listening to their speech and reading some of their compositions, I'm certain they were telling the truth.

The *Washington Star* reported recently that in Montgomery County, Maryland, school authorities, alarmed at declining test scores, decided to screen new applicants for teaching positions. In the past 18 months, 50 percent of those applying to teach English failed a simple, standarized test in grammar, punctuation and spelling.

One of the problems is that we no longer teach one standard correct form of English; we teach *three different types* of English. The "new grammar" textbooks carefully spell out Formal English, Conversational English, and Colloquial English. All three are considered correct and appropriate, depending upon the occasion. Thus, "between you and I" is considered perfectly acceptable under most circumstances. Only in very formal conversations and in literary writings would "between you and me" be preferred. I had quite a provocative discussion one evening at a board meeting with a high school English teacher on just this subject. He considered me highly unreasonable and I am certain most old fashioned when I suggested that he should teach his students to say "between you and me." He even stated categorically that children who are achieving below the 50th percentile cannot possibly be expected to learn this "formal" English!

Why do educators insist on making things so difficult? In the "old days" we used to tell our students that *between* is a preposition and that prepositions are followed by the objective form of the pronoun. *Me, him, her, them.* Not I, she, and they. Difficult? Not at all. With a little practice anyone can recognize a preposition when he sees one. And, unlike many foreign languages, English has only one objective form of the pronoun. The hangup, I suppose, is that those who have never been exposed to such antiquated concepts as diagramming a sentence, haven't the faintest idea what a subject or an object looks like.

This, by the way, probably accounts for another widespread misusage. Somewhere the word is out that if in doubt whether to use *I* or *me,* substitute *myself.* Obviously since there is no such word as *I-self,* no decision needs to be made. Sadly, enough, this grammatical atrocity is not limited to the below-50-percentile set (pardon my new math). In fact, it seems to carry with it some degree of snob appeal. The more educated the speaker, the more likely it seems to appear. I have heard it from the lips of congressmen, senators, and, yes, even school superintendents.

Some years ago grammarians considered splitting an infinitive a mortal sin. Gradually they have sotened this rock hard position and now agree that in certain usages the split infinitive is acceptable. However, this softening should not grant an unlimited license for mass infinitive-fracturing. But this is precisely what has happened, to the great consternation of those of us with sensitive ears. And the sad part is that the fracturers are not even aware of what they are doing. Most of them, in fact, don't even recognize an infinitive when they see one.

And then there is the latest innovation. Bilingual Education. We are told by the experts that foreign students must be taught in their native tongue. Special textbooks must be purchased. Special classes must be set up. Bilingual teachers must be hired. The whole process is developing into a horrendously expensive and largely counter productive, bureaucratic boondoggle.

Any student of language knows without question that the best way to become fluent in a foreign tongue is to live with people who speak it. In this manner, one is forced to communicate exclusively in the foreign language without being able to use one's native tongue as a crutch. No one, I believe, would dispute this. Why then does not this same reasoning apply to foreign-speaking children, living in the United States? Henry Higgins found it to be most effective in creating his "Fair Lady." Remember his technique? Drill. Drill. Drill. Repeat. Repeat. Repeat. In precise, pure, perfect English. Did he speak to Liza in her dialect? He most certainly did not. If he had, he most assuredly would have developed a Cockney accent. And just as assuredly unless they mend their ways so will our modern day educators succeed in degrading the English language even further than it has already deteriorated.

A few weeks ago I read an editorial in a high school newspaper concerning the recent disclosure that at the University of California 52 percent of the entering freshmen are required to take "bonehead" English. The editorial in attempting to whitewash the situation quotes an English teacher as stating, "What does writing a comprehensive paragraph, essay, or even a letter have to do with being a success in life?" In my opinion, just about everything. It's high time educators get back to realizing the importance of having a thorough command of the English language, and once again begin teaching it.

FEDERAL FUNDS

Much has been written about how dangerous it is for school districts to accept federal funds. Most concerns are related to loss of local control, attachment of "strings," and gross inefficiencies due to bureaucratic regulations and bunglings. Very little, however, has been said about the actual damage to the educational process. "Damage"? you say. "How can that be? Wasn't the whole idea behind federal funding to help school districts *improve* the quality of their education?" Yes, of course it was. But can you show me a single statistic, from anywhere in the United States, where federal funding has honestly and significantly improved test scores?

Oh, of course there are examples of limited duration where massive expenditures appear to have effected some short-term improvement. We can point to several such isolated instances in Pasadena. But overall, year after year, in spite of millions of dollars worth of extra equipment and personnel supplied by federal funding, our test scores continued to decline. Each year the administrators and the board of education would examine the horrifying statistics, decide that we needed more money to improve the quality of education, and apply for additional federal funds.

To be specific, in 1968 our district employed one certificated teacher for every 23.2 students. This figure includes only the personnel at each school, not any of the administrators, directors, or consultants at our education center. By 1974, almost entirely because of the introduction of federal programs, this pupil-teacher ratio dropped to 18.5 students per teacher. In addition at each of the federally funded schools, a full-time paid aide was present in nearly every classroom.

Then you should see the new equipment. Tons of it of all descriptions. The "educational" toys we discussed earlier. Games. Puzzles. Blocks. And the more exotic audiovisual equipment. Remedial devices of all kinds. Some of them highly complex and extremely expensive, the so-called "teaching machines." In most of our federally-funded schools a separate room is set aside just to store this material, and special teachers are assigned to catalog, dispense, and collect it as well as to instruct the regular classroom teachers how to use it. We have math labs and reading labs, math specialists, math consultants, reading specialists, reading consultants, and coordinators of all descriptions.

Remedial programs and "proficiency" classes are rampant. At one of our elementary schools an elaborate remedial reading laboratory with 30 reading machines, each costing many thousands of dollars, was set up with federal grants. None of this expensive equipment could possibly have been paid for from local funds, nor would it even have been considered. But with "free" and seemingly unlimited federal resources, such things are easily accessible, simply for the asking. The irony of it all is that every one of these devices is designed to accomplish what the classroom teacher should have done in the first place.

Yet, in spite of all these expenditures, our test scores over this same time period continued to plummet. Fourth grade is a good level to examine, since a massive portion of the federal money was concentrated in the lower grades. In Reading at the fourth grade, our district average percentile dropped steadily from 45 to 33. Spelling, from 42 to 29. Language, from 39 to 26. Could the drop be explained by "bright flight?" Not at all. During the same time that our fourth grade scores were dropping, our first grade readiness tests, a measure of the ability level of children entering school, actually *increased* from the 55th percentile to the 61st percentile.

Without question the largest single complaint I hear from teachers concerns the paperwork involved in complying with the guidelines of the federal programs. Many state quite simply that they spend more time record keeping than they do teaching. The amount of time and money required to develop the application forms and the evaluation reports is staggering. As a new board member, I used to pour over these reams of documents quite conscientiously, and even try to file them. But soon I realized that to do so was physically impossible. Not only was all available storage space soon exhausted, but also no time remained for me to carry out my other duties effectively. This, I suspect, is precisely the same dilemma experienced by the teachers. Unlike me, they are forced to wade through the tons of material in order to be certain that they are complying with the myriads of rules and regulations. More and more of their time is wasted and the children suffer.

Some teachers, of course, enjoy their new role. It's much more fun and far less demanding to pass out games, or deposit a child in front of a "mechanical teacher" than to organize a detailed lesson plan. The new gimmicks are highly tempting. And after all, "If *our* district doesn't accept these gifts from the federal government, some other district will." We should be so lucky!

As I mentioned earlier, much of our federal funding in Pasadena is concentrated in the lower grades. In 1975, we had roughly a dozen of our K-3 schools receiving federal funds in varying amounts ranging from a minimal $27,000 at one school to a whopping figure of nearly $300,000 at two of the others. This is in *addition* to the regular budget at the school which follows the district formula and is uniform at all schools. Each school has roughly the same ethnic makeup. There are some differences in socioeconomic level, but with a few exceptions the variations are relatively minor. At some schools the federal programs have been going on for ten years. At most schools, for at least four or five years. Certainly enough time that an impact should be felt. Our Fundamental schools receive no federal funds to supplement their academic program.

Just for fun I plotted the reading and math scores for kindergarten, first, second, and third grades at each of these schools versus the dollars spent for federal funds. There is some scatter in the data points but the trend is obvious, and can be seen clearly in the resulting curves shown on the following two pages. *The larger the expenditure of federal funds, the lower the test scores.*

If it were not so tragic, the inference would be almost humorous. Maybe I should get on the bandwagon with the good Mr. Parkinson and add for posterity a truism that shall forever after be known as Myers' Law:

Spend enough federal money for education and we can spend our country not only into bankruptcy but also into illiteracy.

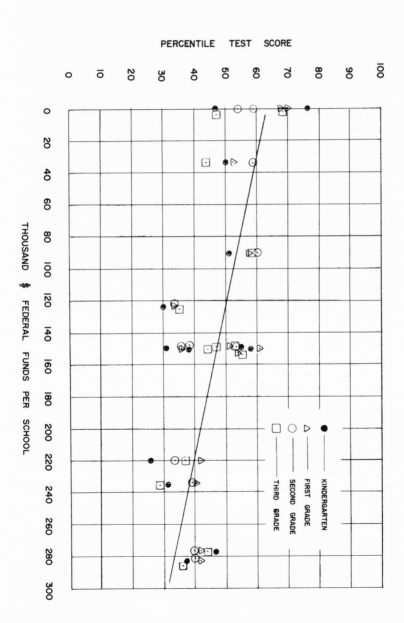

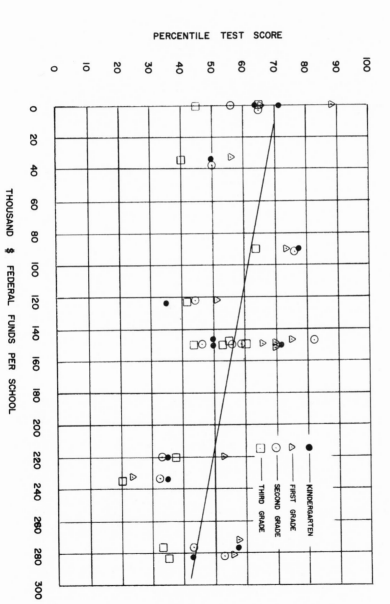

EFFECT OF FEDERAL FUNDS ON PRIMARY MATHEMATICS SCORES
PASADENA UNIFIED SCHOOL DISTRICT ———— APRIL 1975

PERCENTILE TEST SCORE

THOUSAND $ FEDERAL FUNDS PER SCHOOL

KINDERGARTEN
FIRST GRADE
SECOND GRADE
THIRD GRADE

43

TEXTBOOKS

So far most of our discussion about classroom problems has centered around methods and techniques rather than actual content of textbooks. In no way, however, does this mean I am ignoring the problem or downgrading its importance. The time is long overdue for parents to take a critical look at the learning materials being forced upon their children. Unfortunately whenever a parent or a board member complains about a textbook, he is immediately labeled either a prude or an extremist.

Actually there are two types of objectionable textbooks, altough some particularly offensive ones contain the worst features of both. The first is simply the dirty word type filled with four letter words, sex, and violence. Many of our modern works of fiction fall into this category. They are usually found in English or literature classes at the junior high or senior high level as supplementary texts, but sometimes they are required reading. Fortunately they are relatively easy to identify. School board member Alice Moore and her associates in Kanawha County, West Virginia, and the Mel Gablers in Texas have done an excellent job of exposing some of the worst of these texts.

The second type is far more insidious and sometimes much less obvious. There are no four letter words, no sex, no violence. Nothing that might readily be spotted by a curious parent browsing through his child's reading materials. Sometimes books must be analyzed rather carefully in order to understand their true message, which occasionally borders on the subliminal. A little practice, however, soon enables the reviewer to identify the same general pattern in all of these texts. Undermining of the work ethic, family life, parental authority, respect for law and order. Frequently they emphasize unhappiness, dissatisfaction, poverty, and unfair treatment, especially of minorities. Sometimes they are downright morbid. All presumably under the pretense of being realistic and true to life.

Rarely do these textbooks include stories of how Johnny worked his fingers to the bone and subsequently was rewarded for his efforts. Never do they extol the benefits of free enterprise, or the advantages of a capitalistic society, nor do they ever even hint at such a dastardly thing as patriotism. Quite simply, they are always downgrading, always critical, never uplifting or complimentary.

Even if we discount the subversive aspects of these textbooks, nearly all of them possess the common characteristic of being exceedingly dull and uninteresting. Almost without exception the authors are so carried away trying to sway the minds of their young readers to their points of view that they fail to make the material interesting. Of course there are not too many fascinating points to bring up when one is writing about garbage. And, let's face it, most of the authors of these types of stories must certainly be sick, dull, uninteresting characters in the first place.

The net result when these boring materials are shoved into the classroom is simply that even if Johnny *can* read, he most assuredly will have no desire to do so. And if he *can't* read, he is not about to try. In these days of widespread illiteracy among our young people, the uninteresting textbooks are particularly damaging. While I am not advocating pornography as an incentive to entice our young people to read, I could more easily condone a tastefully done story with a bit of spice than one that is purely dullsville. But then my wife always accuses me of thinking more like a man than like a father of three teen-aged daughters — not even to mention like a school board member — so maybe my opinion on this subject is somewhat biased.

Seriously, however, one significant point that may often be overlooked in trying to determine why Johnny can't read may simply be because he has no desire to do so. Obviously in order to read he must first learn the mechanics, but to become truly proficient he must then practice. Forcing him to practice if he doesn't *want* to, requires the dedication of a saint, the patience of Job, and sometimes almost the cruelty of a diligent slave master. Ask any long-suffering parent who has endured the piano lesson experience.

Recently I carefully went through a series of roughly two hundred supplementary reading texts that were up for adoption by our district. Most of them were brand new, the latest offerings by the book publishers. All were expensively done. Lots of pictures. Often in full color. But were they exciting? Would they entrance the reader so he could hardly bear to put them down? Did they even come close, for example, to the adventures of Tom Swift or Laura Ingalls Wilder? Or how about some good mind boggling science fiction or a portion of spine tingling suspense? No! Alas!

For almost all of them, I had to fight to stay awake while plodding through their dull, pointless contents. Almost all were strictly Type II. Not one of them would be capable of causing a child to miss his dinner or stay up past his bedtime. But Tom Swift did. And Robin Hood did. And Robinson Crusoe did, along with hundreds of other classics of the past. It's high time for modern authors of children's books to regain some of the expertise of their predecessors. Maybe, just maybe, when Johnny *wants* to read he *will* read.

III
THE SOLUTION

Anyone can criticize. Finding fault is easy. In fact for many of us the ability to do so seems to come naturally. At times it may even be therapeutic. The seasoned top sergeant, I am told, really begins to worry when his men stop complaining. All of us complain about the weather. About taxes. About politics. About a million things. But very few of us offer any viable alternative to improve the situations we are complaining about.

So it is with the first section of this book. For the most part my thoughts up to this point have been primarily critical. And this is as it should be, because only after we have thoroughly analyzed a problem and specifically identified its causes, can we hope to develop a solution. Nor do I pretend to be omnipotent, capable of solving all of the problems that exist in the field of education. Some of them, quite honestly, I have pondered for many months and I still have no practical answers.

In fact, all too often I am inclined to throw up my hands in despair and simply conclude there is no answer. It's easy to adopt such an attitude. And it's also a good excuse to sit back on one's derriere and do nothing. Merely shaking one's head sadly and lamenting mournfully that public education in America is down the drain, is not the least bit constructive, even though it may be true. If public education is indeed down the drain it simply must be brought back up again — inch by inch if necessary. If America is to survive, there is no other choice.

INVOLVEMENT

First of all, get involved. If my writing up to this point has been even moderately effective, it should have at least aroused your curiosity and hopefully even whetted your appetite to do a little investigating on your own. If you are a parent of a school age child, by all means visit his classroom. Or better yet, volunteer to serve as a classroom aide. For non-parents, too, the volunteer aide route is an excellent way to get started with grass roots involvement. Not only does it provide much-needed help to the teacher but also it offers an ideal means of gaining first hand information about what is happening in that classroom.

Be a double agent. Be useful. Be helpful. Be supportive. But at the same time do a little spying. Don't be obvious, of course. For example, it probably would not be wise to carry a copy of this book with you to the classroom each day. To do so would in all likelihood not endear you to the teachers and the administrators at your school. But *do* study it at home and check for yourself the points I have discussed. Don't simply take my word for them. After a month or two in the classroom you may well be able to add a chapter or two of your own.

Second, start attending your local school board meetings. Often these days we see statements lamenting the fact that only a very small percentage of the voters can remember the names of their congressmen or even their senators. I'll wager that the percentage who can identify the members of their local school board is even smaller. Yet the policies dictated by that board and by thousands of its counterparts all across the country will determine without question whether this great nation will continue to survive and prosper or will deteriorate and die.

Study the members of your board. Identify those who agree with your educational philosophy, if any, as well as those who disagree. Ask questions. Make statements. Always there is a spot on the agenda for audience participation. Make use of it. Don't of course, expect instant response to your pleas. At first you may feel you are being ignored, that you are wasting your time. Be patient. Come back next week with a dozen friends. Hammer away one point at a time. Never flail wildly, hoping to correct all the evils of the district at once. Pinpoint one crucial issue and concentrate on it week after week if necessary, until action is taken. Very few school boards can resist such a concentrated frontal assault indefinitely, as long as it is done in good taste and in a reasonable manner. Always give copies of your statements to the press.

Most importantly, get organized. Start a group of concerned citizens and plan your attack. Find out the date of the next school board election and begin scouring the community for top notch candidates.

Your biggest enemy, by far, will be apathy. Most parents you will find have not the slightest idea what is going on, and many could care less. But a few dedicated ones will rally to your cause — probably not more than a half a dozen who really are willing to work or even become involved. Don't be discouraged by your lack of numbers and don't throw up your hands and quit when many of the helpers you had counted on back out. Resign yourself from the very beginning that a small handful of you are going to have to carry the lion's share of the load. Because you are! Just remember, history is full of instances where tiny groups of dedicated individuals have literally changed the course of human events, often creating shock waves felt around the world. With all humility, since I am one of the persons involved, and with my only purpose being to inspire and assist you in similar endeavors, let me tell you how a group of us here in Pasadena did indeed create such a shock wave.

A BIT OF HISTORY

One fateful evening in the fall of 1972, a group of about a dozen Pasadenans met to discuss the upcoming school board election. The situation was critical. Three years earlier, extensive forced busing had been mandated on the district by a federal judge, and a sympathetic board of education had refused to appeal the judge's decision.

Roughly 7000 students had fled the public school system, nearly 40 percent of the white student population, and the rate of flight was not decreasing. It was estimated that eight to ten thousand children in the area were enrolled in private schools, many of which had long waiting lists. Test scores were plummeting, despite a massive infusion of federal funds, and the rate of decline, like the rate of white flight, showed no signs of leveling off.

Property values were at an all-time low, while similar homes in neighboring school districts were in great demand at premium prices. It was perfectly obvious to anyone who was willing to face reality that Pasadena, the "Crown City" of the West was in deep trouble. The old adage, "As the schools go, so goes the community," was being confirmed once again.

The small committee who gathered together that evening recognized full well that their backs were against the wall and that time was running out. Three seats on the five-man school board were up for election, and all three incumbents were strongly supportive of both forced busing and progressive education. The two remaining seats were split philosophically. One was held by a strong pro-busing advocate, the other by Henry Marcheschi, a lone, outspoken opponent of forced busing.

The committee decided to "go for broke," to try to capture all three seats by running a slate of three candidates. So far so good. But then came the important process of picking the *right* candidates. This stage, for those of you who are considering a similar undertaking, is absolutely critical. Obviously the prospective candidate must first be willing to run. This in itself may require a lot of arm twisting. I remember vividly that when I first was approached I reacted immediately with "A person would have to have holes in his head to run for the school board in Pasadena!" That, by the way, may have been one of the most profoundly true utterances of my entire career.

Mere willingness however, is not enough. While it may be argued with some validity that *anyone* can be elected to public office these days if he has sufficient financial backing, a good candidate certainly makes the process much, much easier. This is particularly true in a relatively small community, where the candidates are known personally, not simply as images on a television screen. By all means don't merely latch on to the first volunteer who offers his services. Set your sights high. Pick the candidate (victim) you want and then plan your strategy for convincing him to run.

Back to history. From that first meeting of a tiny group of dedicated citizens and many subsequent ones, a campaign was initiated that in March of 1973 culminated in the election of our slate, Vetterli, Myers, and Newton (Dr. Richard Vetterli, Mr. Lyman Newton, and me), to the Board of Education of the Pasadena Unified School District.

We were elected in the primary, but did not actually take office until July. This gave us four months to think, to plan, and to become acquainted with hundreds of details and personalities. The more we studied, the more frustrated we became. At one point Dr. Vetterli exclaimed, only partially in jest, "I've just decided it's too late. There is absolutely nothing we can do!"

All of us knew, however, that something drastic had to be done. Immediately we initiated the legal machinery to try to reverse our court order and "stop forced busing." But we recognized that such an appeal would take many months, maybe even years. Pasadena simply didn't have that much time. What could we do in the meantime to reverse both the mass exodus of students and the declining test scores? What was it that the private schools could offer, many of them operating on a fraction of the budget of our public schools, that we could not? My wife and I debated this subject hour after hour. Finally, like one of those light bulbs that appear in cartoonists' sketches, the idea of our Fundamental School emerged. My life has not been the same since.

ALTERNATIVES

Educators, I am forced to admit, are always busy. They are never willing to accept the status quo. While their motives may at times be open to question, no one can doubt their zeal. Look at their track record over just the past quarter century. Think of all the wonderful new programs that have been proposed. All highly touted. All claimed to be the panacea that would solve the educational ills of the world. Look-say reading. New math. Learning stations. Team teaching. Diagnostic and prescriptive techniques. Individualized instruction. Manipulative aids. All sorts of innovative educational "experiences." As soon as one of them falls into disrepute under a barrage of complaints from unhappy parents another is quickly introduced. The latest? Alternatives in education.

All children don't learn in the same manner, we are told. We must provide alternative methods of instruction. It would be futile to point out that since its birthday two centuries ago America has produced a population with the lowest rate of illiteracy of any nation on earth. And it has done so with a single, basic type of educational curriculum, namely emphasis on the fundamentals, the three R's if you will, in orderly, well disciplined classrooms. But let's not cloud the issue with facts. The educators' minds are made up. Their heads nod up and down sagely whenever they get together at one of their innumerable conferences or in-service training sessions. Yes. We must provide alternatives.

And provide alternatives they have! But all of them of the same type. All over America, open-structured alternative schools have been springing up. The "schools without walls." Schools where the classroom is obsolete.

Children learn, (supposedly), by experiences, by field trips, by communing with nature, rather than by drill, by memorization, or by any type of structured program. There are no grade levels and no grades. Informa;ity is the rule. Teachers insist on being addressed by their students on a first-name basis, and commonly attire themselves in a manner designed to help them "relate" to those students. Direction, order, and discipline, as I define them at least, are completely foreign to the alternative school. Basically, I am told, the children decide for themselves, with a minimum of influence from the staff. Recently I read a quote in a local newspaper on the subject that made me chuckle. An irate parent is alleged to have said that the term "alternative school" should be replaced with "alternative *to* school."

We have such a school in Pasadena, started several years ago by the former board of education as a pilot program in cooperation with the University of Massachusetts. Quite honestly, I would not permit my children within three miles of it. To me it is utter chaos. My first inclination, upon being elected to the board was to recommend doing away with it as quickly and as mercifully as possible. But the more I thought about it, the more I rejected the idea.

Pasadena, unlike the commonly painted picture of it, is no longer composed primarily of conservative little old ladies in tennis shoes. The presence of a local university, plus several other colleges in nearby communities, as well as various other reasons, have caused the influx of a significant and sometimes highly vocal liberal element. Many of these progressively oriented intellectuals are fully convinced of the merits of a permissive educational approach. Pasadena has had a long and colorful history of battles between conservative and liberal educators. Each time the liberals gained control they threw out the conservative programs, and vice versa. In fact this yo-yo effect has been going on for years, through cycle after cycle. Why repeat the process once again by closing the alternative school? Why not instead open a structured school at the other end of the educational spectrum and let the two schools compete? After all, conservatives believe competition is healthy, and lack of competition is disastrous. Why not test this philosophy in our public school system by providing more than one alternative?

THE REBIRTH OF FUNDAMENTAL EDUCATION

In July of 1973, a tiny seed was planted that was destined to initiate the Phoenix-like rebirth of fundamental education in Pasadena and set an example for the entire nation. The raging fires of permissiveness and progressiveness had taken their toll, and the wreckage of what was once the finest educational system in the country lay smoldering in ruins. Could it be rebuilt? The only way to find out was to try.

At our first official business meeting, the newly installed board of education announced that if there was sufficient demand a fundamental school would be opened in September for kindergarten through eighth grade. My wife and I, as well as my three teen-age daughters, plus various teachers, administrators, and other interested persons had spent weeks talking over how to set up such a school. Imagine the thrill and the challenge of being able to custom design the ideal public school of one's dreams. After years of complaining about the system, here was a chance to change it.

But then, why simply imagine the thrill we felt in Pasadena? Why not embark on a similar endeavor in your own community? Unless, of course, you are completely happy with your school system the way it is. Fortunately, as of this writing at least, every town in America still enjoys sufficient freedom for you to proceed. Dozens of citizens' groups are already doing so. In fact, scarcely a day goes by when I am not asked for advice by some such organization. Therefore I will attempt to make this next section as complete as possible. Hopefully, it can serve as a step-by-step "Instruction Manual for the Do It Yourself Fundamental School."

Our first press release was as follows:

THE FUNDAMENTAL SCHOOL

For many years, Pasadena has promoted new and innovative ideas and concepts in its school system. Currently, in addition to the many state and federally funded programs, we have the Alternative School, Evening High School, and Foothill High School. Next year, at the elementary, and possibly the junior high level we propose to add the Fundamental School.

Admission to the Fundamental School will be purely voluntary. The average cost per student will be lower than in the conventional school at the same grade level. There will be no federally funded programs.

The attached pages describe the basic philosophy of the Fundamental School. Other policies will be established as the school develops.

FUNDAMENTAL SCHOOL REQUIREMENTS

Admission to the Fundamental School may be obtained by written application from the parent or guardian. The parent or guardian must agree to accept the rules and regulations of the school before the application of his child will be considered. There are no minimum ability standards, but IQ and achievement testing will be required prior to admission.

Teachers and administrators may apply for assignment to the Fundamental School. In order to be considered, they must agree to the rules and regulations of the school. If at any time a teacher or administrator violates these rules or regulations he may be reassigned to the regular school program.

FUNDAMENTAL SCHOOL FEATURES

1 *Emphasis will be on fundamentals: reading, writing, arithmetic, discipline, and respect. Art, music, and physical education will also be provided. Reading will be taught strictly by the phonics method. Traditional, basic mathematics, not "new math" will be utilized.*

2 *Homework will be assigned in each basic subject, at every grade level, on a regular basis.*

3 *No child will be passed on to a higher grade until he has mastered the minimum requirements set for his grade level.*

4 *Achievement and IQ testing will be performed upon admission to the School and periodically thereafter. Parents will have access to the results of these tests.*

5 *Classes will be ability grouped.*

6 *Strict discipline will be maintained. The teacher is authorized and expected to maintain order in the classroom. Paddling and detention are permitted at the discretion of the teacher.*

7 *Parents or guardians must agree to meet with the teacher periodically, at mutually convenient times, to discuss the progress of the child.*

8 *Letter grades will be given periodically in each of the basic subjects.*

9 *After-school help with homework will be provided where required.*

10 *Dress, for both students and teachers, must comply with minimum standards. Neatness and cleanliness are mandatory.*

11 *High moral standards, respect, courtesy, and patriotism will be emphasized at all grade levels.*

Immediately our opposition swung into action with the standard delaying tactics. "How can you start a brand new school without first setting up a committee to study it?" they asked. "You have to schedule meetings, with community input. Call in experts and consultants to give their opinions. Set up a pilot program on a small scale at one of our existing schools and study the results for a year or two before proceeding on a full-sized venture. You don't have any evidence whatsoever that such a school will work." To which we calmly replied that fundamental schools have been studied and proven on this continent alone for well over two hundred years. Only when educators strayed from basic fundamental precepts did they get into trouble.

Fortunately our board majority was determined to proceed. We realized that a delay would be disastrous for two reasons. First and foremost, another year would be lost before we could hope to reverse the downward trends in the district. Hundreds more Johnnys would not learn to read, to write, or to behave. Hundreds more would flee to private schools or neighboring communities. Second, in a year, dozens of reasons could and would be concocted to show "conclusively" that such a school would not work. So despite the objections, early in June we voted four to one to send a questionnaire to all kindergarten through eighth grade parents asking if they were interested in enrolling their children in the proposed fundamental school. A copy of that original questionnaire is shown in the section entitled "A Guide to Starting a Fundamental School."

It should be noted that we did not give a great deal of specific information about the school. In particular we did not mention its location. We wanted to be certain that parents enrolled their children because they believed in the fundamental concept and not because of some extraneous benefit.

Within three weeks more than 3500 applications flooded into Ed Center, including about 130 from parents of children in private schools. Roughly 30 percent of the applications were from minority parents.

We were absolutely ecstatic, of course, but at that point we really faced a problem. There were only about six weeks left to start a brand new school. In that short time we had to select a staff, set up the curriculum, clean and repair the site (a former junior high school, closed because of loss in enrollment), complete a million details and *finally,* select the students.

We could only take about 1000. Because of our court mandate the school had to be racially balanced. Thus we could not simply adopt a first-come-first-served procedure. Also, because we did not want to be criticized for taking only the good students, we attempted, by examining test scores, to make the school representative of the achievement level of the district. This was no small task, and in any community even slightly less explosive than Pasadena, I would not recommend such an effort.

Most of the work of setting up the school fell upon the shoulders of three or four dedicated and capable persons. Our superintendent, Ray Cortines, gave his support and helped select the principal, Dr. Mike Kellner, but for the most part the superintendent quite understandably was far too busy worrying about all of the other schools in the district to be able to spend much effort on the new fundamental school. Willard Craft, assistant superintendent, and Anna Mary Hession, director of curriculum, along with Doris Hendin, the assistant principal, and Dr. Kellner carried most of the load.

Many others, including the custodians and the maintenance men, performed admirably. They didn't appear to mind the hard work and the long hours. Somehow they seemed to sense the fact as they painted out the graffiti, repaired the dented lockers, replaced the torn off towel dispensers, and scrubbed the restrooms that *this* time they would stay that way. Even the mutilated bust of John Marshall was given a new arm, a new nose, and a shiny coat of paint. He sits proudly once again in a place of honor at the entrance to the auditorium.

Nearly everyone seemed to become infected with the spirit of the operation. Without a doubt the most important task was the selection of teachers from the list of volunteers. Here the many years of experience of Mrs. Hession and Dr. Kellner played the key role as they interviewed the applicants.

Next came the monumental task of going over the list of students and making room assignments. Each class had to be balanced, roughly at least, with proportionate numbers of boys and girls, as well as with the proper ethnic ratio. We also attempted to ability-group the classes, studying the test scores of each student.

At the junior high level, seventh and eighth grades, the problem was even more complicated, because classes were not self-contained and scheduling had to be arranged. Also provisions had to be made for at least a limited number of options and electives. In addition, activities such as sports, shop, music, and student government had to be provided.

Often when I visit other communities I am asked the pros and cons of starting a fundamental school at the elementary level versus starting one at the secondary level. Because of their own horrendous experiences in the junior and senior high schools, parents sometimes want to jump into that area with both feet and ignore the elementary grades. This is wrong for two reasons. First of all, the source of almost all of our educational and disciplinary problems occurs in the first few years of school. If the elementary schools do a proper job, many of the difficulties never develop in the high schools and those that do arise can be controlled because the children have been properly trained. Second, establishing a fundamental secondary school requires several orders of magnitude more effort and expertise than does starting an elementary school. In normal circumstances, phasing in the high school a grade or two at a time, after first setting up the fundamental elementary school, would probably be advisable.

In any event, for better or for worse, in September of 1973 the John Marshall Fundamental School, kindergarten through eighth grade, opened its doors. On the evening before the opening day, an orientation meeting was held for parents. It was a proud day for many of us. The school was squeaky clean. Floors were waxed, restrooms were scrubbed. Teachers were dressed as though they were attending a wedding reception. My wife even provided a bouquet of flowers for the entry hall. "Overdone," you say. Well maybe just a bit. But after years of famine a tiny amount of overeating is understandable and excusable.

That was the beginning. None of us even in our wildest dreams had any idea that night what we had done, what an impact we were about to produce. In just a few weeks word of our school spread like a wildfire through tinder-dry grassland. Requests for information starting pouring in. "Send us complete details about your fundamental school," they pleaded. "We need one desperately in our district. Our children aren't learning to read, to write, to perform the simple functions of mathematics, to behave. When can we come to visit your school? Could you come to speak to us?"

At first we kept up reasonably well with the requests, but then the national publications got wind of our operation. *Time, McCalls, Newsweek, The Wall Street Journal, Readers Digest,* to name a few. Max Rafferty wrote a story about us in his syndicated column. Dozens of newspapers all across the country as well as in Canada and even in Europe picked up the trail and suddenly we literally became inundated.

Dr. Kellner, the principal, bore the brunt of the barrage. Nearly every weekend and any weekday evening he could be found in his office answering requests for information. During the school day he served as tour guide for the constant stream of visitors. And in his "spare" time he managed the school.

Eventually we were forced to restrict visitors. Wednesday was designated as visitors' day and appointments were set up weeks in advance. As a rule of thumb we try not to schedule more than 30 or 40 guests on any particular Wednesday, but on occasion this guideline is unavoidably violated. Also, it is not always possible to adhere strictly to the Wednesday rule. Special VIP requests sometimes just cannot be ignored. The net result is that rarely does a day pass without at least one visitor.

At latest count we have processed more than a thousand requests for information. I myself have received several hundred. Just for fun we tabulated the geographical distribution. Nearly every state, including Alaska, is represented. Apparently the educational problems we are experiencing in Pasadena are duplicated all across the country.

Everywhere parents groups are forming and are requesting their local school boards to set up fundamental schools. Often our new-found friends with whom we have corresponded send us newspaper clippings reporting their progress. For this I am grateful.

An editorial in the Lompoc, California *Record* proposed a definition of a Fundamental School. I like it so well I have adopted it as my own.

A Fundamental School is simply a school where basics of education are stressed with little or no experimentation; where discipline reigns and patriotism flourishes.

Nations Schools and Colleges entitled their feature story on our school, "The New Conservative Alternative." I like that too.

Fundamental Schools are springing up all across the country. A grateful parent in Palo Alto sent me a clipping describing how a school was started there. Let me share it with you.

Are parents interested in schools with calm and orderly classrooms?

All over America parents are showing their desire and demand that their children begin to receive a basic education in an atmosphere of order and respect. There is such a public school in the Bay area, the Hoover Elementary School in Palo Alto.

A group of parents there who wished their children to escape the "innovative, experimental" programs petitioned the Palo Alto school board for a Fundamental School. A modest notice for registration for such a school was issued. Was there a market for such a school? Anxious parents brought their sleeping bags and thermos bottles against the 4:30 a.m. chill for the 8:00 registration for the chance to enroll their children in a school where they could be taught reading and writing and arithmetic in "calm classrooms." Twenty minutes later registration was closed — with a waiting list larger than the number admitted.

In Pasadena, too, our waiting list refused to decrease. At mid term that first year we admitted an additional 200 students. Next year, in the fall of 1974, we added a high school, grades nine through twelve, at the Marshall site, and opened a second fundamental school, this one kindergarten through sixth in another section of town. This school, Sierra Mesa, had been recommended for closure by the superintendent because of declining enrollment. When school opened, much to our amazement the district enrollment, instead of declining twelve to fifteen hundred students as it had done each year for the past five to six years, actually *increased* by about 600 students! Both fundamental schools were full, and we *still* had nearly twelve hundred applicants on the waiting list.

This points out a significant phenomenon. Because of our court-ordered racial-balance requirement, and because Blacks did not sign up for our Fundamental program in as large numbers as whites, the waiting list has always been predominantly white. Before our Fundamental Schools were opened, whites had been fleeing the district in large numbers. Now, they were practically breaking down the doors to enroll in a racially balanced, 40 percent Black school! All of which demonstrates clearly that white parents are perfectly willing to send their children to schools with Black children and Black teachers if they are convinced that the school is providing top quality education in a safe, well disciplined environment.

The Fundamental Schools in Pasadena *are* safe, and parents know it. Of course no one can *guarantee* that there will never be a racial incident on Fundamental School premises. But after three years of operation, none has occurred. In fact, no serious altercation of any sort has been experienced. This is particularly significant since a number of the initial enrollees were sent there by parents, and sometimes by principals, who had literally given up trying to discipline a particularly difficult child and sent him to Fundamental as a last resort.

A principal of a regular elementary school confirmed this one evening by unexpectedly jumping to my defense when I was speaking at a PTA meeting. "You only took the good kids," a teacher said to me accusingly. "Anyone could make *them* behave." "Not so," said the principal. "I literally rubbed my hands in glee when several of our little darlings left to go to Marshall." She went on to tell about one specific child who was a real terror. Always out of control. Always sent to her office for one reason or another. Completely incorrigible. Several months after he had been sent to Marshall, he returned to his old school one evening with his parents and a younger brother and sister for an open house. During the teacher's presentation he listened quietly, and then stayed patiently at his parents' side as they wandered about the room. Finally the incredulous principal could contain herself no longer and said to the boy, "Johnny, it's so nice to have you back visiting us this evening. I can't help but notice how well behaved you are." To which the boy replied, "Well you see, I go to the Fundamental School now. They don't *let* us misbehave at the Fundamental School." Sometimes it's just as simple as that.

Occasionally I am asked what we do with the hyperactive child at the Fundamental School. Usually I double-talk a bit. I guess I'm just a bit chicken to take on the experts and say flat out that I question whether hyperactivity is an inborn condition or one that has developed because of lack of discipline. At the very least I suspect that many so-called hyperactive children could be "cured" in the same manner that worked so effectively with this particular Johnny.

In no way do I mean to suggest that we never have problems at our Fundamental Schools, that things are always perfect, that the children always behave like angels. Nor would we necessarily want them to. School would be a pretty dull and listless place if all the students were merely robots. This of course is precisely the picture that opponents try to paint of a structured program. Our students at Fundamental, like students everywhere, are alive and vibrant. They are told what they *can* do and what they *cannot* do. But occasionally they forget and break one of the rules — or possibly do so intentionally as a calculated sort of risk just to test the system. Children from time immemorial are experts in this field, by the way. Always probing and testing to see just how far they can go, how much they can get away with before they are restrained.

Naturally, at Fundamental we don't like to admit to outsiders that things are ever less than perfect. Wednesdays my wife frequently serves as tour guide. One day she was leading a group of visitors through the building when she spotted a rather large piece of paper on the floor. Hoping the guests hadn't noticed, she unobtrusively leaned over, picked up the paper, and stuffed it in her pocket. Some time later, after the visitors had been safely sent on their way, she cautiously pulled the paper out of her pocket and read, neatly written 25 times, "I will not chew gum in class." But worst of all luck, the poor, unfortunate, gum-chewing student had signed his name at the bottom of the page. This simply delighted good natured, fun loving but firm, Dr. Kellner. "Come back tomorrow," he told my wife. "I'll have a second paper for you written by our friend that says, *I will not throw paper on the floor!*"

Some of my readers may say, "All you tell us sounds very impressive, but what about the children? Don't you care about their feelings? What do *they* think about the school?"

First of all, let me say that I do *not* believe, as permissive advocates try to convince us, that the "inmates should run the institutions." Not only do we adults have the right, but also the *obligation,* to determine how our children should be educated — and it is bloody well high time we start assuming that obligation. The very idea of expecting an elementary school child to choose his own curriculum is patently absurd. Even at the high school level we adults must set the basic requirements. A major problem today, in our schools as well as in our homes, is that children have far too many choices, far too much freedom, far too many liberties, and far too little *direction* from their elders. Certainly after decades of experience in the "school of hard knocks" adults should have better insight concerning what is best for their children than the children themselves.

Noah Webster once said, "The command to honor your father and mother comprehends not only due respect and obedience to your parents; but all due respect to other superiors. The distinction of age is one established by God himself, and is perhaps the only difference of rank in society which is of divine origin. It is a distinction of utmost importance to society, it cannot be destroyed, and it ought not be forgotten."

But unlike Noah Webster, our modern liberal philosophers tell parents they must treat their children as equals. Never tell a child he must *obey*. Reason with him. Expose him to all sides of every question. Make sure he reads all about communism, socialism, and atheism as presented of course by the communists, the socialists and the atheists, as well as about capitalism, free enterprise, and belief in God. Then, completely on his own, free from any parental influence whatsoever, let him with his inexperienced immature mind make his own choice. In simple words, forget the lessons of the past. Ignore the experiences of former generations. Start afresh with each new generation.

At the Fundamental School we discount this philosophy completely. This does not mean that we are insensitive to the feelings of our children or that we ignore their input. We recognize that if a child is unhappy something is wrong and we try to correct the situation — not necessarily by giving him his own way or by letting him do as he pleases, but by deciding, after weighing all the factors, what in our mature, adult opinion will best satisfy his needs. We do indeed direct our children and we try to influence them. Each morning we have character-building sessions to teach them what they *should* do and what they should *not* do. We teach them pride. We teach them respect. We teach them to behave. And, yes, we teach them to love their country. To let them recognize its mistakes, of course, but to condition their minds so that they constantly want to build and improve upon the solid principles that have caused our great nation to grow and prosper.

We keep them busy. Almost never are they left to "do their own thing." This does not mean that we spend every minute teaching the three R's. Sports, music, drama, art and science all are vital in the development of a child. And none are neglected at the Fundamental School.

We also teach our children to be polite, to be courteous, to be considerate. At lunch time, teachers and aides are constantly on the lookout for poor table manners or infractions of etiquette. Grammatical errors are corrected not only in English class but also on the playground, in the music room, or in the lunch line by all of the staff, not only by the English teachers. You would be amazed how this keeps the teachers as well as the students on their toes. Imagine how embarassing it would be for a teacher to be caught by his students in a grammatical boo-boo!

Competition is fostered not only in sports but also in academics. Math contests and spelling bees are common. Last year, one particularly confident sixth grade class challenged the twelfth graders to a spelling bee. The seniors, wisely I think, chickened out. But until the day of their graduation they never heard the end of it from the sixth graders!

"But you still haven't answered our question," you say. "What do the children really think about the Fundamental School? Aren't they disturbed by their structured, disciplined environment? Don't they miss being allowed to do what they want to do?" Almost without exception, the answer is a resounding NO. Occasionally a child misses some former classmates or some particular activity, primarily at the upper grade levels and asks to return to his regular school, but the percentage of such requests is infinitesimal. Overwhelmingly the exact opposite is true. The children *love* their new school and are highly enthusiastic about it.

About two months after Marshall Fundamental opened, one of the fifth-grade teachers had her children write a short theme telling what they thought about their school. All of their writings follow the same basic pattern. Let me share some excerpts with you. The copies reproduced here are from the original rough drafts, complete with mispellings and grammatical errors. The later revised and corrected editions are much improved technically, but far less colorful. At the risk of incurring the eternal wrath of our fine Fundamental staff at Marshall, I chose to use the original unexpurgated manuscripts.

COPIES OF CHILDREN'S THEMES

John Marshall School
Grade 5, Room 219
November 14, 1973

John Marshall fundamental school is a very good school. I would like to tell you about it. Last year I went to ▭▭▭ School. I left there because I thought there was to much fighting. I am glad I left. We do all kinds of fun things and ofcourse the adults are a little stricter, but that helps a lot. I think there should be more schools like it It is a very well organized school too. I am glad that I'm here, I like it! I want to stay a long time.

I think this is the best school I have every went to. I went to two other schools but this is the best so far. See me and my mother want me in the best school we can find. It is diffent then the others you don't just set all day long and never learn anything and they don't just give you a paper and say do it in 5 minutes. what they do here is diffent they give you lots of work but they give you directions on how to do it I love my knew school and it looks like evry one that goes here dos too.

I'd like to tell you what I think of
this scool. I'm excited all the time of
what we're going to do becase I always
know we're are going to do it without a lot of talking. At my other scool
most of the kids would talk back to the
teacher with bad words and there was 1 to 3
fights almost ever day. At this school
theres usually never ever a fight. We always
learn alot too. there are some bad points
about the school too, but then Almost
Everything has bad points but the best
thing of the scool is almost everybody
do'es there best for the scool to make it
work out very good. Those are some
of the points I wanted to bring out to
you.

I would like to tell you a bit about
are School. I like to come to school,
last year I went to [A PRIVATE SCHOOL]
School. I did not like to come to the
School last year. what I like a bout
John Marshall School is that the teacher
is very strict on us that I like last
year they let us eat in class and
chew gum and eat candy in class and
to much fighting and I all most got
ekckspell from school.

I like John marshall. I feel that I am going to learn more this year than I leared last year becase last year we moved class around it was fun moveing class around but every body wants to do fun things and not do school work, so this is what I mean. we moved class around one teacher would have to get use to us and we would have to get use to them And if we would not have to move around the teacher could find out better what we know and what we don't know. And there is lots of other things I could tell you but it is all most time to go home so I will tell you one more thing that there is Not very many fights at this school. I have not seen one yet.

I think John Marshall school is better then any other School I have been to. I met ten new kid in one day. At our School we do lots of fun things in math, spelling, and even history is fun the forth fifth and sixth grades haven't had many fights yet at ▓▓▓▓▓▓ there were two or three fight a day. we get more work done here and almost every teacher is nice.

John Marshall is real fun I'm gone to have real fun at John Marshall School. I'm learning to read now to. And to do math. I couldnt do it before.

My name is Elizabeth. Marshall School is a very nice school. And strick. And I like strick schools. When you go to a strick school you learn a lot. I hope you tell other's about our school. And if you ask me I would Recommed your children to our school.

So you see, our children are *crying* for discipline. They are also crying to learn. And, just like adults, they feel good when they *have* learned something. They are tired of being told they can do whatever they want, and they are bored wuth playing games. It's high time we adults do something about it.

THE RESULTS

"The proof of the pudding is in the eating." It's great to theorize, to talk about the wonders of fundamental education, but is there any really good hard data to support the claims? Yes, indeed there is. And with each passing day the results become more-and-more conclusive.

Since 1969, the Pasadena school district has carried out an extensive test program. To spread out the work load, grades one through three are tested each spring and grades four through twelve each fall. Therefore, shortly after school opened in September of 1973, all grade four through twelve students were tested, including those in grades four through eight at the newly established John Marshall Fundamental School.

Results of those 1973 tests showed a continuation of the downward trend that had plagued the district (and hundreds of other districts) for years. Fourth grade was a typical example. Since 1969, district-wide reading scores had declined from the 45th percentile to the 33rd percentile at an alarmingly consistent rate of about three points each year. Spelling dropped from 42 to 29 percent, language from 39 to 26, arithmetic from 37 to 29. There was no sign of any upturn or even a leveling off. Entering first graders, however, were still testing at the 61st percentile, eleven points above the national norm, with no sign of any decline. This would indicate that the problem lay in our school system, not in a deterioration in the capability of our students.

During this same period we had lost nearly 7000 students, at a steady rate of about 1200-1500 students each year. And again there was no indication that the flight was tapering off. It was estimated that 8000-10,000 students were enrolled in private schools in the area.

Could the declining test scores be attributed to an insufficient number of teachers? Hardly. Largely because of a massive infusion of federal funds, exceeding a quarter of a million dollars at some schools, we had a few more teachers in 1973 than in 1968 when there were 7000 more students. In fact, the average student-teacher ratio, counting principals and other certified administrators at each school but not at Ed Center, had dropped from 23.2 to 1 in 1968 to 18.5 to 1 in 1973. In addition, more than 400 full-time classroom aides had been added at the schools, again almost exclusively with federal funds. And of course many classrooms also had volunteer aides as well as a goodly supply of practice teachers.

Educators and politicians alike constantly talk about the need for reducing class size. It's like being for motherhood. It's also mighty expensive. While it obviously is desirable to strive to keep classes as small as economically feasible, our plummeting test scores in Pasadena could in no way be blamed on an insufficient number of teachers.

The point is further illustrated by some recent test data for Vietnamese children now living in Oceanside, California. As reported in *The New York Times*, some 33 of these elementary and secondary-school children were given standarized achievement tests. In arithmetic computation, the average Vietnamese pupil scored at the 93rd percentile, while the average Oceanside pupil scored at the 29th. In arithmetic concepts, the average Vietnamese pupil scored in the 95th percentile, while the average Oceanside pupil was in the 24th percentile. In the application or usage of basic skills, the average Vietnamese scored in the 91st percentile, while the average local pupil scored in the 35th.

It was noted that most of the Vietnamese children were considered average pupils in their native country, and were the sons and daughters of fishermen, farmers and clerks. They had attended schools in Vietnam that

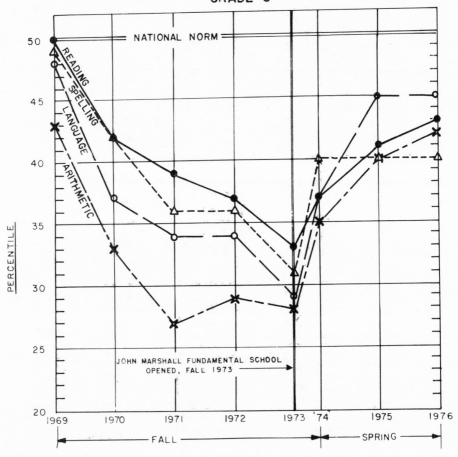

DISTRICT MEDIAN TEST SCORES
PUSD, 1969 – 1976
GRADE 6

had 60 to 90 pupils per class. In Oceanside, a middle-income predominantly white community, a class of 30 is considered large.

That first year of the Fundamental School the board and the administration really cracked the whip. We announced that all students would be retested in the spring just before the close of the school year. I remember quite vividly making a presentation at a packed board meeting of the statistics just noted here, plus other equally alarming ones for other grade

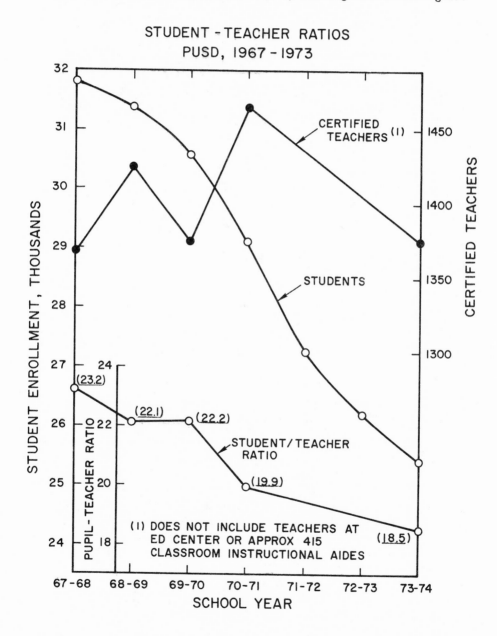

STUDENT - TEACHER RATIOS
PUSD, 1967 - 1973

levels, and concluding by stating that if the spring scores did not show significant improvement, the board would be taking a long hard look at programs, policies, *and personnel* before the next school year.

The spring scores *did* improve, far beyond our wildest dreams. We *expected* improvement at the Fundamental School, and we were not disappointed. But we were not prepared for the effect the good old free enterprise competition that the Fundamental School provided had upon the regular schools. For the first time public schools in Pasadena were forced to compete. And compete they did! Sixth grade scores are plotted on the following page. A dramatic rise in all areas. For the elementary grades, where we had been experiencing the three point decline per year discussed previously, the district-wide average score increased eight points! Marshall Fundamental led the way with a whopping 12 points! At the junior high level, scores at the regular schools stayed just about constant, ranging from a one point decrease to a two point increase. Marshall Fundamental, however, jumped seven percentile points.

Enrollment, like the test scores, also reversed its downward spiral and shot upward. Nine hundred students came back into our public school system from private schools of which only about half could be explained by the closure of one particular private school. Roughly 450 of these private school students enrolled in the Fundamental School. Suddenly we had a new problem. One that Pasadena had not faced in nearly a decade. We had to hire extra teachers and provide additional facilities, above our planned budget allocation, to accommodate the increased enrollment.

Sierra Mesa school had been recommended for closure by the superintendent because of declining enrollment. Instead of closing it, however, in September of 1974 we opened it as a K-6 fundamental school. It was immediately filled to capacity. As a regular K-3 school, Sierra Mesa had been about average. The last year of its operation as a regular school its first grade reading scores averaged at the 39th percentile. Math scores, at the 36th percentile. After its first year as a fundamental school, the corresponding first grade scores skyrocketed to the 78th percentile in reading and the 81st percentile in math!

Admittedly these were not the same students, but remember the statistics quoted earlier which showed that scores of entering first graders of all of our schools had not changed appreciably in several years. Minor variations could be attributed to possible differences in student abilities, but certainly not the spectacular gain actually experienced.

Many teachers avidly declare that the teaching of reading at the kindergarten level should not even be attempted. Kindergarten, they say, is strictly for adjustment, for play, for happy experiences. Certainly not for teaching academics. At Sierra Mesa, after its first year as a fundamental school, 50 percent of the kindergarten children were reading at the second grade level.

In an earlier chapter we discussed at length the cumulative achievement deficit of minorities in our public schools, particularly Blacks.

Coleman recognized this, attributed it to segregation, and advocated busing to solve the problem. After five years of busing in Pasadena, the gap between Black and white test scores had not narrowed one iota. At the Fundamental Schools, however, this was not the case.

Black trustee John Hardy and white trustee Dr. Richard Vetterli made an in-depth study of the situation and released their findings to the local press. Some of these findings are as follows:

In the first grade at Marshall Fundamental School, the 1975 test results showed that Black students averaged at the 69th percentile in reading and at the 54th percentile in math. In second grade, they scored at the 62nd percentile in reading and at the 66th percentile in math, all far above the district average for Blacks. At Sierra Mesa Fundamental School after its first year of operation, first grade Black students reached the 60th percentile in both reading and math. These scores for Blacks, Hardy pointed out, are practically the same as the overall district average of 65 for white students, illustrating that Blacks with proper instruction can achieve equally with whites regardless of differences in socioeconomic status. District-wide, however, Blacks at this grade level scored at a dismal 27th percentile.

Students in one second grade class at Marshall, with slightly more than 50 percent Black enrollment, achieved an average of nearly 25 months academic growth in just 10 months.

Students in grades one, two, and three at Marshall, more than 40 percent of whom are Black, topped the national norm in every class in reading and language. These high results, incidentally, were achieved despite the fact that 52 percent of Marshall's students come from homes where the annual income of $10,000 or less, and more than 28 percent from homes where the annual income is less than $8000.

At Sierra Mesa Fundamental, where 42 percent of the students are Black, 83 percent of all students scored above the national norm in first grade reading and 76 percent of all students scored above the national norm in first grade math.

Hardy concluded that at the fundamental schools Black students are contributing to the higher test scores, unlike in the district as a whole where Blacks are generally well below the norm. He continued by saying emphatically that busing has not produced academic improvement for Blacks and that until fundamental schools were introduced in Pasadena the disparity between Black and white achievement actually *widened* under the busing program. "The whole purpose of busing was to close the gap," Hardy said. "But only in the Fundamental Schools has the gap narrowed. And that is not because of busing, but because of the type of instruction."

The "in" thing these days among educational statisticians is to attempt to correlate test scores with socioeconomic level. The implication is that students can't learn because they are poor. Admittedly, there does seem to be a relationship. No one, however, seems to have considered the "chicken or egg" possibility that people are poor because they are uneducated, not uneducatable because they are poor.

In any event the test scores from our Fundamental Schools are throwing the socioeconomic correlations completely out of kilter, as can be seen in the following table.

1975 TEST SCORES — MEDIAN PERCENTILE Comparing Sierra Mesa Fundamental School with Audubon School of Higher Socio-economic Makeup and a Control School with Similar Socio-economic Makeup (Scores indicate the exact center of distribution with 50 percent scoring above the number and 50 percent below.)			
	AUDUBON	SIERRA MESA	CONTROL SCH.
READING			
K Prereading	49	77	47
Grade 1	41	70	42
Grade 2	34	54	44
Grade 3	45	68	49
LANGUAGE			
Grade 1	60	68	46
Grade 2	29	64	42
Grade 3	39	64	43
MATHEMATICS			
Grade 1	51	89	58
Grade 2	35	56	44
Grade 3	31	65	33
SOCIO-ECONOMIC DISTRIBUTION			
FAMILY INCOME RANGE	AUDUBON	SIERRA MESA	CONTROL SCHOOL
$ 8,000 or Less	1.5%	13.2%	24.0%
8-10,000	9.0%	23.1%	12.6%
10-14,000	70.0%	37.3%	46.9%
14-16,000	8.7%	19.8%	16.5%
16,000 and above	10.8%	6.6%	0.0%

Not only did the test scores at Sierra Mesa Fundamental School far exceed those of a control school with a similar socioecomic level but also they greatly surpassed those of a second school having a much *higher* economic population.

Admittedly our test results are somewhat premature. Several more years at least will be required before the evidence becomes conclusive. But the trends already established are overwhelmingly on the side of fundamental education. A reversal of those trends appears to be highly unlikely.

THE OPPOSITION

"Opposition," you say. "Surely you can't be serious. Your Fundamental School is completely voluntary. Only those parents who want structured education for their children apply for admission. Those who prefer open structure can go to your alternative school. Or the middle grounders can remain in the regular schools. You tell us also that the cost per student is lower at the Fundamental School than at any of the other schools in the district. Teachers too are at the Fundamental School purely on a voluntary basis, because they choose to be there. How an anyone object to such an arrangement?"

Alas, although your logic is entirely reasonable, the Fundamental School in Pasadena has become the most controversial school in the district. Its creation, in fact, was one of the major issues, charges if you will, in the unsuccessful recall attempt against Dr. Vetterli, Mr. Newton, and me. Chief among the opponents are the teachers' unions, especially the more militant ones. Why? Quite simple. Most unions protect incompetent teachers. Fundamental schools expose them. The extent of this opposition has become almost paranoid. Rarely does a school board meeting go by without some derogatory statement, often a formally prepared one, against our Fundamental program.

Recently I was invited by the superintendent and the board of education of a small rural district in northern California to visit them and speak about our Fundamental School. This, by the way, was the first time a group of school *administrators* rather than a committee of concerned parents, who contact me by the dozens, has expressed a need for starting such a program.

Somehow word of my visit was relayed to the teachers, who came out en masse to heckle my most uncontroversial speech. Several weeks later when several of our top administrators were invited by this same district to follow up my talk with specific details, the opposition flew two of their people 500 miles to attend the meeting. I am happy to report that their efforts were unsuccessful. The proposed fundamental school is now in operation.

Yes, word of the fundamental school movement has reached the major teachers' unions. They see it as a real threat. They don't like it. And apparently they are willing to go all out to try to stop it.

Always there are exceptions. Many of the lesser known teachers' organizations and thousands of our finest teachers are squarely behind the return to fundamental education. Recently I spoke to a national convention of the National Educators' Fellowship and was enthusiastically received. The National Association of Professional Educators, NAPE, has also been most supportive of the fundamental school concept.

A second group of individuals is working desperately to see us fail. Hopefully they are small in number. Some of you readers will doubt that they even exist. Not too long ago I probably would have agreed. But time and time again, rationalize as I may, I cannot come up with any other logical reason for their activities. This is a group of power-hungry individuals who simply *do not want the masses to become educated,* especially the minorities. An educated electorate votes intelligently. It cannot be led around. Whether this conspiracy is international or strictly local in its makeup is open to conjecture. But I am convinced it exists and it must be recognized if it is to be defeated.

Finally, there are those poor misguided souls who have been so brainwashed about the glories of progressive, permissive education that they are dedicated to inflicting their views on everyone else. And they are completely intolerant of the idea that parents who don't buy such pablum should not have it forced down their throats.

Let me quote from a "fan" letter I received from a gentleman at a well known graduate school of education on the East Coast. I have no way of knowing whether the writer is a student or a professor.

Dear Sir,

I have just finished reading an article about your "back to basics education," and find it hard to believe that you would publicize your narrow views of education.

You justify your actions based on a claim that the waiting list for your school has passed the 1000 mark. The waiting list I can believe, because people such as yourself have made parents afraid, and thus they are pushing for the three "R's." I can understand a parent's lack of knowledge on progressive educational techniques and their confusion, but your lack of intelligence has amazed me!

Do you really believe that a child with so much to look forward to thinks that happiness is manners because you tell him so? I for one do not!

Happiness for a child in today's schools is being an individual learner. It's this individual learner and not the parents nor the community, that should be considered the primary client of the schools and he should be given the greatest possible choice and responsibility in charting his or her educational passage.

While basic skills in reading and computation should not be neglected, a "new curriculum" is needed, not a tradition-oriented education. This new curriculum should emphasize such matters as social relationships, decision making, career preparation, the use of leisure time and esthetic awareness.

In closing I would like to point out that through a program as yours, you are doomed if not today then tomorrow, to be plagued by school violence and vandalism, as well as by student boredom and academic failure. Maybe only then will you realize that educational progress depends more on the student's "demonstrated competence" rather than on time in class and you will broaden the learning opportunities for your children beyond the dull, rigid and ineffectual confines of tradition or a building.

Sincerely,

A bit scarry, isn't it? Think how many other sincere, dedicated persons all across America share this gentleman's philosophy. And thousands more of our youth are being taught it daily as gospel at our universities and teachers' colleges. Don't simply assume that the pendulum is swinging away from permissiveness and back toward structured basic education. I think it is. But only with a great deal of effort will it come even close to reaching its goal. Never underestimate the opposition. It is battered, bruised and reeling from its repeated failures, but in no way is it ready to lie down and surrender.

THE CHALLENGE

If you have come this far in my book, assuming you aren't one of those cheaters who starts by reading the last chapter first, you probably agree with many of my points of view. Otherwise you would long since have turned too purple to continue. Most of my readers, I suspect, will either strongly agree or violently disagree.

To those who disagree, my apologies for disturbing your digestive juices. Go back to reading about the wonders of progressive education. Don't worry about running out of material. Books on the subject outnumber books like mine by at least five hundred to one. But beware! In Pasadena we've thrown down the gauntlet. Our forces are small but they are spreading rapidly. Our backs are up against the wall. We fully realize that we are engaged in a life-or-death struggle. If we should lose, there will be no second chance.

To those who agree, agreement is not enough. Accept the challenge and do something. Turn off that television set. Forget about that golf date. Become an activist. Organize a group of parents. Assign members to study every school in your community — in detail. Ask to see the test scores. Go over all of your children's textbooks, word for word. Delegate responsible representatives from your group to take turns speaking at school board meetings and analyze the actions of the board carefully.

Demand a return to basic fundamental education. This book will give you sufficient ammunition for dozens of broadside volleys against the opposition. Hammer at them with facts. Politely, of course, but again, again, and again.

Some board members will be sympathetic from the beginning. Others will cave in under your constant barrage, and some will have to be replaced. Plan that replacement carefully with the cool, calculated cunning of a panther stalking his prey. Remember, the tide of public opinion is with you, and it is growing stronger and more powerful with each passing day. Already I know of at least a score of candidates who have been elected to boards of education this past year on one simple platform — back to basic fundamental education. It can happen just as easily in your community.

Won't you accept the challenge? If you do, your life, like mine, will never be the same. But I promise you the thrill of accomplishment of working on a project that is absolutely essential for national survival is one that you will never forget.

Much as I hate to end this section with a somewhat overworked phrase, nothing else seems to be quite as appropriate. Yes, accept the challenge. Get in the fight.

The nation you save may be your own.

IV
A WORD OF ADVICE

This chapter is in effect an epilogue. I am composing it nearly two years after writing the rest of this book and nearly four years after the conception of John Marshall Fundamental School. Hindsight is always superior to foresight, and experience, without question, is hard to surpass as a teacher. Therefore, with all due humility, I feel both qualified and obligated to pass on a few choice words of advice to those who just now may be embarking upon a course in their own communities that we in Pasadena began four years ago.

During the past four years we have constantly attempted to identify both our strengths and our weaknesses and have made many changes. In addition, I have received hundreds of letters and phone calls from persons in other districts, telling me their problems and asking questions about our program. Finally, I have spoken to more than a hundred audiences in dozens of communities and a score or so of states and in so doing have received broad input concerning the educational system in America today.

The most significant observation that I can make from my experiences is that wherever I go, educational problems are almost identical. In fact, when I go into a completely strange town and am met by a citizens' committee I can almost always tell them about their community. A fortune telling, crystal ball type of thing. Always my new friends are absolutely amazed. They think I must be psychic. Actually it's as simple as catching fish in a barrel and sort of a game for me. The names, of course, are different, but the cast of characters and the plot are always the same. Let me tell you the story, "The Perils of Education in Anytown, USA."

The natives are restless. Johnny can't read. Johnny can't add. He rarely brings home any homework. There is little or no discipline in his classroom. His parents are upset. They talk to other parents and compare notes. They form a committee. They hold meetings. They have heard about the back to basics movement and they write to Pasadena for information about the John Marshall Fundamental School. Sometimes they invite Dr. Myers to come speak to their group.

Always they appeal first to their superintendent, who, by the way, is a master at dealing with restless natives. His first approach is to try to convince them that they do not have a problem. "We are not like Pasadena," he says. "We have always taught the basics. Our children are learning to read, to do math. We have no discipline problems." Sometimes this tack works, but almost always there are enough case histories and testimonials contradicting his statements that he is forced to go to Plan II. Plan II is usually successful in at least providing a delaying action. "Fine," says the superintendent. "We'll form a committee and study the situation." This is a very clever move. First of all, it convinces the restless natives that the administration is on their side. Second, it creates at least a six-months delay even with a completely dedicated, hard-working study committee. Finally, by loading the committee with a few strong opponents, the whole process can be stalled indefinitely.

This committee stacking is a favorite ploy. Even though the committee is charged to study how to implement a fundamental school, the administration will insist, "All sides must be represented. We must be fair and objective, you know." The net result, chaos and disaster.

Another sabotaging technique the administration may use is to insist that the committee come up with minutely detailed plans and policies for the proposed fundamental school. This, itself, can require years of debate and discussion, and then once the document is finally prepared, it can be taken apart, bit by bit, by the opposition.

Eventually the natives realize that the administration is really not friendly at all. But often, time has run out. Their members have become discouraged and tired. They pack up their drums and quietly steal away to their homes.

Another approach, which can sometimes be used concurrently with the one just described, is to work on the board of education. Usually this is completely futile because in spite of the fact that the school board theoretically runs the district, such is rarely the case. Almost always, the board of education is little more than a rubber stamp for the superintendent.

In most districts, one board member is supportive of the fundamental concept. Sometimes a second member is at least lukewarm to the idea. Almost always one is violently opposed. And the other members don't really know where they stand. However, when an actual vote is taken, the majority will go along with the recommendation of the superintendent.

By far the most violent opposition comes from the teachers' organizations, most of them are almost paranoid in their fight against establishing a fundamental school. Often I am asked why this is true. In Pasadena, for example, in the past four years the Fundamental Schools have attracted more than 1800 students back to our public schools from private schools or from other districts. This saves a considerable number of jobs, supposedly a primary concern of a union organization. We lean over backwards to make certain that fundamental schools receive no special favors. The budgets at fundamental schools are the lowest in the district.

Why then the big fuss from the unions? There may actually be no valid reason, but reason or not the opposition is very real, well organized, and difficult to combat.

There you have it: "The Perils of Education in Anytown, USA." The cards are stacked. Without question, it is difficult to beat the establishment. But it can be done. It *is* being done in scores of communities all across America. I personally know of dozens of fundamental schools that have already been established and many more that are on the way. Last year in San Francisco I spoke to a lady school board member from Philadelphia at a back-to-the-basics seminar. She went home and started not one but seventeen fundamental schools in Philadelphia.

I could go on with many more success stories. I could also tell of many failures and frustrations. The important point, however, is that it *can* be done. It has been done. It must be done.

One major stumbling block seems to be choosing a site for a proposed fundamental school. If an empty facility is available, as was true for our original Fundamental School in Pasadena, there is no problem. But when this is not the case, how does one proceed?

Typically, most communities select the most "basic" school in the district for the proposed fundamental school. Usually the principal and often many of the staff are believers in fundamental education, so it is reasoned that a minimum of change will be required. Sometimes this plan is successful, but frequently there are a few parents or teachers who are adamantly opposed to the idea and argue that their rights would be violated if they needed to leave their school because they didn't approve of its new "fundamental" policies. It is absolutely amazing how an overwhelming majority is often controlled by an infinitessimal minority! But such, unfortunately is true.

One other objection to choosing the most basic school for the fundamental school is that as far as the welfare of the overall district is concerned, the school that is already the "healthiest" is receiving the most medication.

Geographical considerations often are a factor. Busing is sometimes involved if children need to be transported from their neighborhood school to a new fundamental school in another part of town. In Pasadena, by court order, we bus roughly half of our children each day for ethnic-balance, so busing to the Fundamental School presents no particular problem or added expense. Other communities, however, often do not want to provide the additional transportation.

In several districts, parents who volunteer for the fundamental program are required to provide their own transportation. Normally, I am told, they are so happy to have the fundamental school that they are perfectly willing to do so. Car pools are utilized widely so that the inconvenience is not intolerable. I do not object at all to this approach. After all, if these same children were attending private school their parents would be responsible for their transportation. In fact, I look forward to the day when school districts can *get* out of the busing business and back into the business of educating children.

Probably the most commonly considered compromise is to establish a school within a school. Instead of converting an entire school into a fundamental school with the inherent tactical problems just outlined, why not simply designate several classrooms at a regular school as fundamental classes? Obviously the mechanics would be much simpler and there would be far less disruption.

For a long time I strongly opposed this approach. "The fundamental concept is an entire program, not just a classroom technique," I reasoned. "What happens when the fundamental children who have been taught courtesy, pride, respect, discipline and structure go to lunch or meet in the halls or on the playground with children who have been indoctrinated with the permissive, unstructured, do your own thing philosophy? What happens when the child who has been taught not to throw paper on the floor, to write on the walls, to kick in the lockers, meets the child who could care less? What happens when these two diverse groups of children are mixed together in the auditorium during an assembly or at a school dance or at an athletic event?" How can a principal be both "structured" and "unstructured," a fundamental believer and a disciple of John Dewey and Dr. Spock? Obviously there is a dichotomy. The situation is far from ideal.

However, I have mellowed a bit, partly because of pure pragmatism but partly because I have seen the idea work in several instances. Several conditions should be insisted upon however, if such a plan is considered.

Ideally, some physical barrier should be present in the building to separate the two schools. A separate wing, for example, or a separate floor could be utilized. While complete isolation is normally not possible, or maybe not even desirable, lunch times and assembly programs should be staggered. I say, *not even desirable,* for somewhat of an ulterior motive. If the school is run properly, and the administrators are chosen wisely, I am convinced that the fundamental philosophy will ultimately rub off on the non-fundamentalists. I know of two specific schools where this has happened. But.. beware! The reverse could also occur. So, while if I had my druthers I would still prefer the pure fundamental school to the mixed bag of a school within a school, I would go along with the latter, if the former was not possible. Half a loaf is better than none.

When I am asked about parental involvement, I have some mixed emotions. In Pasadena, parents do not run the Fundamental Schools. We do not have, nor have we ever had, a parent curriculum committee or a parent advisory committee. Contrary to popular belief, parents are probably less involved at Fundamental Schools than at most regular schools. The PTA's while highly supportive, are not normally involved in policy matters. Our professional administrators are in charge. They carry out the policies established by the board of education. They plan the curriculum. They are responsible and accountable for the performance of the school. This, I believe, is as it should be.

In Pasadena, however, we have an ideal, although undoubtedly a most atypical, situation. The Board of Education is solidly and unanimously behind the Fundamental concept. Since the Board approves all administrative appointments we can be sure that administrators at the Fundamental Schools are strong proponents of the Fundamental philosophy. The administrators, in turn, choose their teachers. It's as simple as that. Or at least it *should* be. Myriads of roadblocks constantly seem to loom up along the way; *people* problems, not *philosophy* problems, are always the major stumbling blocks.

In other districts the situation is usually somewhat different. Most successful fundamental schools are greatly influenced and strongly monitored by the parent group who started them. This is necessary because the boards of education and the school officials are merely *tolerant* of fundamental schools, not particularly supportive of them. So, while I am inherently wary of schools that are run by non-professional parent committees, I can well understand that in some situations it may be necessary. After all, the professional educators have made quite a mess of things for the past couple of decades. The parent groups could hardly help but be an improvement.

Ideally, however, the only real solution for parents who are unhappy with their schools and want to do something about it, is to gain the support of the board of education. If board members are not supportive, the cold, hard fact is that they must be replaced. Any lesser efforts, such as trying to work with school officials and convince them of the need for a fundamental school, are almost always a complete waste of time.

Admittedly, the ballot-box procedure is a slow one. It may take several years, and it most certainly will require many hours of hard, dedicated work and planning. Parents often are reluctant to accept this long-range approach. They want immediate action, so they opt to work on the present administrators. While no harm is usually done and in some rare occasions positive results may be achieved, until the board is strongly supportive, the major result is usually frustration after frustration.

The ballot-box approach often poses a major difficulty. Parents of school-age children who are most greatly concerned, are normally completely uninformed about politics. They have no idea of how to run a political campaign. School board elections are notoriously unorganized. They are, of course, nonpartisan and rarely provoke any strong, organized group backing a particular candidate. I was horrified when a dozen or so candidates ran for one or two seats in several nearby communities. Many of the candidates were friends and had no particular philosophical disagreements. Most were unhappy with the schools, some for different reasons, such as high taxes, but none had any community-wide support. The net result: a weak campaign, a vote split, and a win for the incumbents.

For my final bit of advice, let me pass on a few thoughts about how to elect good school board members. While this book is in no way intended to be political, one should never apologize for discussing politics, nor for becoming involved in politics. It is in fact when good people do *not* become involved in political activity that government deteriorates.

First of all, become informed about your local election rules. Commonly, school board members serve four-year terms, but elections are held every two years so that all seats are not up for election at once. Sometimes each seat represents one particular area of the district but usually a candidate must only reside within the district not in a particular location to be eligible for a specific seat.

Choose your candidates wisely. Set your sights high. Rarely pick the first person who eagerly volunteers. Invariably he will not be electable. Start with a broad-based committee to study and discuss possible candidates. Involve well known civic and business leaders as well as organizations, such as the Chamber of Commerce. Ask them for suggestions. You are choosing persons to run for an office that may well have more influence on future generations than any other job in America today. While it may be true that a good poltical machine can elect almost *anybody* to office, a top-notch candidate makes the process a lot easier. Remember, once you *do* get him, or her, elected you're stuck for four years. So makes absolutely certain you know what he stands for before you commit yourself to an endorsement. Check into his background thoroughly. Dig out all the skeletons. If you don't, your opponents will. Without question the opposition will try to pin the radical right-wing extremist label on you. Avoid any candidate who could even have the slightest taint of right-wing association, even though he might otherwise be highly qualified.

Second, find a good, capable and experienced campaign manager. In almost every community at least one willing and eligible person exists. Let me tell you about ours in Pasadena: Mrs. Stuart (Gene) Wiberg, housewife. A walking dynamo and a veritable living encyclopedia completely knowledgeable about the minute details of every city, state, and national political campaign for the past twenty years. Knows the life histories of everyone in town. Dedicated. Tireless. Works because she believes in the cause and, although she wouldn't admit it, because she loves it.

Do some hunting in your town. You probably won't find a Gene Wiberg but chances are if you search hard enough you may uncover a reasonable substitute. If you locate the ideal person, my next advice will not be needed. Your campaign manager will already be well informed. But just in case your organization is a bit weak in experience, although strong in enthusiasm, here are a few pointers:

You will need money. Lots of it. Select a finance chairman along with a committee to work on the problem. If at all possible pick a prominent, highly respected citizen to write a finance letter soliciting contributions. List the names of your most influential supporters on the finance letter. Make the letter short and to the point but be certain to mention the key issues of the campaign. Follow up your letter with personal phone calls by members of the committee. Remember, people don't part easily with their money. You'll have to work on extracting it. Along with the finance letter, include an endorsement form to be signed and returned, authorizing that the contributor's name may be used in the list of supporters that will appear later in your advertisements.

Next you will need a brochure. Shop around for a sympathetic printer who will give you a good price, but don't skimp. Make your brochure attractive. Hammer away at key points, the need to return to the basics, for respect, for responsibility, for discipline. Point out that your children aren't learning to read, to write, to spell, to perform the simple functions of mathematics. Locate statistics on test scores, costs, and tax rates in your district. All are public knowledge and must be made available on request. The cost per pupil is often shocking. Compare it with tuition at local private schools and corresponding test scores. Talk with some principals of these private schools. You may find, as we did, that when the public school children take the entrance exam for private school they invariably are put back at least a year.

Select a chairman to arrange speaking engagements at service clubs, civic organizations, and private homes. Let the candidates speak in front of a group of friends before sending them out to face the public. Pretend you are the "enemy." Ask tough, nasty questions. Then analyze the answers. Go over the issues again and again. Remember, you are a fundamentalist: Drill. Drill. Drill. Practice. Practice. Practice.

Keep your opponents on the defensive. Point out constantly all through the campaign that they oppose fundamental education. They will deny it, of course, and make excuses and rationalizations. But don't let them wiggle out. Hammer away at their record, especially at their opposition to providing a back-to-the-basics program in your school system.

Don't overlook your local newspapers even if you think they may be unfriendly. Ask the editor and the publisher if they would meet with your candidates and discuss issues. Remember, very few businessmen today, especially in the newspaper industry, are not painfully aware that Johnny can't read, Johnny can't write, and Johnny can't spell.

Any political expert knows that elections are won in the precincts. There is no substitute for personal contact. In my own first campaign, where Dr. Vetterli, Mr. Newton and I ran as a team, each of us spent every weekend for nearly three months ringing doorbells, sometimes even in the rain. Just for fun I wore a pedometer during these excursions and chalked up a total of 96 miles for the cause. Believe me, this sort of exposure pays off, and incidentally is for the most part surprisingly enjoyable. One thing I learned is never to turn my back on a dog, especially a weimaraner! I still have the teeth marks to remind me, in the unlikely event that I might someday forget.

Finally, on election day get out the vote. It's absolutely amazing how forgetful and irresponsible people can be when it comes to exercising their voting privilege. They need to be prodded again and again.

Divide your district into zones and get the voter precinct sheets from the last election. Try to assign at least one volunteer to each precinct. They are responsible both for distributing literature and for phoning voters a day or two prior to election day and on election day, itself. Don't put too large a load on any one individual. Forty or fifty names per person are all that should be assigned, if you expect an effective job. Your workers should check the voting lists on election day afternoon to see who has not voted, then give the non-voters a reminder phone call. Ask if they need transportation. Keep working until the polls close.

"A lot of work," you say. You'd better believe it! But there is no other way. The stakes are high. The futures of your children and of children yet unborn are on the line. Good Luck.

V
APPENDIX

During the four years since the birth of the John Marshall Fundamental School, I have received a wealth of material from other communities, usually from parent groups, trying to start a fundamental school in their district. I am including some of this material in the Appendix, as well as material from our own district, with the hope that it may serve as an "idea bank" from which others can develop policies and guidelines for their own fundamental school.

The items are not arranged in any particular order. Some have been abstracted to avoid duplication. In a few instances I have made some modifications because of personal preference or experience.

PASADENA UNIFIED SCHOOL DISTRICT
SIERRA MESA FUNDAMENTAL SCHOOL
Allan G. Burt, Principal

Sierra Mesa Fundamental School is designed to give students a thorough grounding in the fundamentals of education. It is a school which was created out of the desires of parents who want the best possible education for their children.

In addition to academic excellence, we are interested in fostering high standards of behavior. We believe that students should act and talk like ladies and gentlemen. Rudeness and discourtesy are breeders of disrespect. We expect all students to treat each other as they want to be treated, with kindness, understanding, and respect.

Last but not least, Sierra Mesa Fundamental School is dedicated to teaching moral and spiritual values, patriotism, and respect for our cherished democratic traditions and institutions.

In order to be successful at Sierra Mesa Fundamental School, we suggest the following:

1. *ATTENDANCE* - One of the most important factors influencing achievement is attendance. The best teacher in the world cannot teach a student who is not present in the classroom. If an absence is unavoidable, it is the student's responsibility to make up work missed.
2. HOMEWORK - Homework will be assigned in each academic subject. Parents are encouraged to check each assignment before it is turned in.
3. *HOME-SCHOOL* - Students whose parents show an active and supportive interest in their school work generally achieve success at school. This interest can be be demonstrated by the parent backing the school and supporting reasonable rules and regulations.
4. *DRESS* - It is our assumption that how a student dresses can affect attitudes toward learning. Dressing in "play" clothes has a tendency to result in "play" attitudes. We encourage students to dress in their best "Sunday-go-to-meeting" clothes. Girls may wear long pants in rainy/cold weather.

Parents who send their children to Sierra Mesa Fundamental School do so of their own free will - it is a choice offered by the Board of Education. If at any time the parents find that the policies of Sierra Mesa Fundamental School are unacceptable, they should request that their children be transferred to their regularly assigned school at the proper time.

Among these policies are the following:
1. Parents must agree to meet with the teachers periodically at mutual convenience to discuss the progress of the student.
2. Strict discipline will be maintained and the teacher will have the authority to conduct the classroom in such a way that learning takes place. In order to reinforce the teacher as an authority in the classroom, the administration will employ such measures as corporal punishment, after school detention, and suspension.
3. Parents will be informed about the misconduct of their children. Frequent or serious offenses may result in transfer or expulsion using the standard guidelines of the District.
4. Students must master minimum requirements in order to be promoted to the next grade.
5. Grades will be issued periodically and will reflect achievement, not effort.

FUNDAMENTAL SCHOOL
SOUTHERN CALIFORNIA

GENERAL RULES: RESPECT, COURTESY, HIGH MORAL STANDARDS. These attitudes can result only if discipline and order are an effective ground rule for the school. Respect and courtesy indicate a conscientious regard for another's needs, feelings, and opinions. Respect and courtesy must first be taught at home and secondly reinforced at school. It is vitally important that this be a two-way street. The example of teachers and to a lesser degree that of the student's peers, plays an important part. Another part of respect and moral standards is reflected in the presentation of class materials, and in attitudes of clothing and grooming. Children need the security of common sense moral standards of right and wrong. Continual change and lax rules lead to insecurity and irresponsibility.

PARENTAL RESPONSIBILITIES: Parents are expected to cooperate with the school in the areas of dress, discipline, and health habits. Parents encourage children to take responsibility for their homework. Religious and moral training is the responsibility of the home. Parents should feel free to confer with the teacher at any time on any subject concerning the child. The responsibility for basic behavior development rightfully belongs with the individual and his parents. The school will not accept sole responsibility for the actions of students. Parents should assist the school in promoting and maintaining acceptable social and moral standards of conduct.

SCHOOL RESPONSIBILITIES: In addition to the regular report card and conference periods, parents will be contacted — and should feel free to contact the school personnel regarding their concerns. Calls and written communications should be directed to school personnel. Appointments should be made — then kept or cancelled — for personal visitation to the school campus.

ENROLLMENT: Entrance is voluntary with no ability requirement; however, achievement testing will be performed upon admission and periodically thereafter, according to Alternative Education Law Sb 445. Students and their parents must agree to support the stands and goals of the program. If parents or students find this difficult to comply with, there is no obligation to attend beyond the given period of time of one semester. They are then free to transfer out of the Structured School program. Applications are accepted on a first come, first served basis.

P.T.O.: A school Parent-Teacher Organization has been formed and notices will be sent periodically. Support of our P.T.O. is encouraged!

SCHOOL LUNCH PROGRAM: Those parents who wish their child to come home for lunch should send a written request to the school. All other students will remain on the campus during the entire lunch period. Students eating at school are to bring a sack or box lunch each day. Students will be able to purchase milk at school so thermos bottles are discouraged due to the possibilities of breakage.

PLEASE LABEL YOUR SACK LUNCHES AND LUNCH BOXES WITH FIRST AND LAST NAMES! Classes will not be disturbed to deliver forgotten lunches. Parents delivering forgotten lunches may leave them in the school office.

The students will eat in an assigned area, separate from the regular school students, or walk home (with written permission). All students in grades one through six will be eating together. They will have separate play periods for grades one to three and four to six.

CURRICULUM: The curriculum for the Structured School has been expressed in a curriculum guide which includes a listing of the materials to be used in 1976-77. It is available for review from the school office.

EMPHASIS ON BASICS: Emphasis on the basic foundations and mastery of skills necessary for an academically sound education includes: reading, with emphasis on phonics, arithmetic, mathematics, English grammar, geography, history, government, penmanship, spelling and science. Art, music, and physical education will be provided. The curriculum goals of each grade level will reinforce, and build on, the previous year's work. Adherence to strict correlation and continuation of subject matter grade by grade is an important feature of this program. There will be a student council that will coordinate the daily recitation of the Pledge of Allegiance.

DRESS: The teachers and staff will dress in an appropriate and acceptable manner, befitting their profession, remembering the example they set is the example the students will follow. For all teachers, the attractiveness and appropriateness of the dress for the occasion will be the key. Their hair and/or beard will be neatly trimmed and will reflect the high standards as established to set an example for the students at the Structured School.

All students are expected to have high standards of appearance and appropriate dress. Their dress should reflect the respect, pride and standards of the student's home and community. A student's dress and general appearance should not be of such extremes that it draws undue attention to the student, nor should the dress and appearance distract or interfere with the teaching and learning in the classroom. All students are expected to wear shoes at all times. Shoes appropriate for PE activities should be worn, or available, at all times. Hair must be clean and combed. Hats may not be worn in the classroom or office. If the shirt is straight across the bottom, it may be worn in or out.

HERE IS A GENERAL RULE: When the type of clothing that is worn draws undue attention to the person wearing it, it is inappropriate for school dress.

It is always nice to sit next to someone who looks good, smells good, and is good. Students and parents should make sure that cleanliness, health and safety are guides to acceptable school attire.

BUS CONDUCT: The rules of the school extend to all transportation to and from school. Students will be provided with the rules of bus behavior by the teachers and drivers of the buses. A bus safety program is scheduled for all classes. Students are expected to be prompt and orderly at all times. Students who miss a bus should go directly home or to the school office - to arrange for transportation. Students are not allowed to ride a different bus with friends unless they have the *written* permission of *both* children's parents.

Each student who rides the bus to school is accountable to the driver of the bus for proper conduct and behavior. Infractions of bus safety and conduct rules will result in a bus conduct report given to the school office by the driver. Violations may result in denial of transportation. In this regard, it should be noted that under the Education Code denial of transportation in no way absolves the student from complying with compulsory attendance laws.

ARRIVAL AT SCHOOL: Children are not to arrive before 8:20 — or their bus time. They are to meet and wait in front of the A-Wing rear entrance. The duty teacher will meet the children at the bus stops and direct them to the playground area. No children are to be on the school grounds before school starts unless a teacher is on duty. Kindergarten children are to go directly to their playground.

DEPARTURE FROM SCHOOL: Each teacher will lead his class to the front of the school where the duty teacher will take them through the gates. Any student who lives north of school may be dismissed to exit at the rear of the school. Students will not be excused from school during the school day without written consent of the school office.

TARDINESS: Tardiness is not excused. Unless very late, children will go directly to their classrooms. The teacher will notify the office of those children who report late. Parents will be notified of unexcused tardiness. Please send a note if there is a reason for arriving late. Students will report directly to the school office if school has been in session for more than fifteen minutes.

OFFICE VISITS: Only those students who have important business are to be in the office. Parents visiting the office should dress as they would for any other business appointment. Visitors must report directly to the Principal's office.

NOON TIME: Students are to stay out of the halls during the lunch hour unless they have a hall pass from their teacher, or are on their way to or from home for lunch. Students may not go to another student's house for lunch without the written permission of *both* students' parents.

All food must be eaten in the lunch area, not on the playground or in any other area. Do not litter the lunch area. No one will be excused until all litter is picked up around the eating area.

Once a student is seated he must remain seated. Seats cannot be changed unless permission is granted by the lunch supervisor.

No P.E. equipment is to be in the lunch area.

Students going home for lunch will need a written note stating what days they are permitted to go home. A second note would be needed for any exceptions.

HALLS: Children are not to walk in the halls, or units, during class time unless they have a hall pass or note from their teacher. No waiting for friends in the halls or units. No running is allowed.

LIBRARY: The library is a place of quiet activities, a learning center with reading research tools, and educational games. Its hours will be scheduled. Each teacher will instruct their students in its use. A librarian is on duty and in charge.

IDENTIFICATION: Students and visitors to campus are requested to reply with their full name (first and last) when addressed.

AUTHORITY: The principal's, teacher's, secretary's, custodian's and noon supervisor's word is final in all matters pertaining to the safety of the children. Their directions are to be followed.

SELF-CONTAINED CLASSROOMS: The classes are conducted in separate, single graded classrooms with one teacher responsible for the maximum of twenty-nine students.

DISCIPLINE: The school philosophy was described in the Alternative School Plan received at the time of enrollment.

The major responsibility for student behavior lies with the parents. In the classroom discipline is firm, but no stricter than necessary to maintain a good learning situation. Sensitivity to the student's feelings with recognition of individuality will be maintained along with firm discipline.

Effective learning cannot function without a positive program of disciplined environment. The Structured School will hold the students responsible for their actions and will protect the student from the individual whose behavior continually disrupts an effective learning program.

In matters involving student behavior that may be used to suspend or expel a student, either presently - or subsequently - from a class, school, or the district, parents or guardians will be notified and involved in all disciplinary procedures.

In the event of an infraction of the school rules, the teacher will speak to the student. Necessary steps will be taken to remedy the situation. In the event that is unsuccessful, the teacher will refer the student to the principal. The principal will notify the parent/guardian of the student.

The notice shall be given in whatever manner is feasible under the circumstances, including, but not limited to, personal contact, telephone contact, written contact.

The notice shall contain the following basic information:
1. Student name, with reference to the incident or infraction and date.
2. A general statement of the incident or infraction.
3. A statement of the time and place at which the informal hearing regarding the infraction, or incident, will be considered.

ABSENCE: When a student is absent from school for any reason the student *must* have a written note, stating the reason for the absence, the dates of absence, and signed and dated by the parent/guardian.

FUND RAISING: The sale, or solicitation, of any item for, or by, students must be coordinated with the school office and the Policy and Review Board.

CARE OF FACILITIES AND MATERIALS: Students will be held responsible for items lost, destroyed or damaged. Teachers will routinely survey the condition of books issued to the students to insure their care.

SCHOOL SUPPLIES: Respect and care is developed through ownership. Students will be asked to provide/purchase basic materials such as pencils, erasers, binders and lined notebook paper.

TEXTBOOKS: Basic textbooks, in the hand of each student, are mandatory as they are the physical approach to problems already solved, documented and preserved.   *HOMEWORK:* When homework is assigned by the teacher it will be meaningful and realistic. Drill in fundamentals may be a feature, but unproductive busy work is not assigned. All assignments will be designed to strengthen daily work, such as arithmetic drill work, book reports, special projects relating directly to subject matter; and should be made with specific purpose and expectation. Homework aids in learning to work independently and to improve skills taught in the classroom.

Parents need to provide a quiet place for the student to work, and a time to work. Homework will not be assigned over weekends. Homework assignments should be of such length that they can be completed within one hour.

GRADING SYSTEM AND REPORTING TO PARENTS: Communication to parents regarding their children's progress is the purpose of conferences and/or report cards. It is the intent of the staff of the Structured School to adopt for the 76-77 school year only, the existing report card forms. This form will be supplemented with conferences and a written comment clarifying the marks of the cards.

Grades will be given in all academic areas for Effort and Achievement. The grades given grades four, five and six will be:

A — B — C — D — FAIL

In Art, Music and PE the grades will be:

O - Outstanding

S - Satisfactory

N - Needs to Improve

U - Unsatisfactory

Grades given to grades one, two, three - and kindergarten will be:

O - Outstanding

S - Satisfactory

N - Needs to Improve

U - Unsatisfactory

A STRUCTURED PRIVATE SCHOOL
ORANGE COUNTY, CALIFORNIA
CURRICULUM

The emphasis at this School is in providing a strong academic foundation. We teach traditional subjects and make every attempt to choose the most direct and logical methods for communicating these subjects. We use phonics in the teaching of reading. Arithmetic is taught by the traditional methods in kindergarten and the early grades until the child has thoroughly mastered the four basic arithmetic operations and all the facts.

History and Geography are taught as separate graded subjects beginning in the third grade. Both are taught at all grade levels from a traditional, patriotic point of view.

We have a half day of academic kindergarten.

HALF-DAY ACADEMIC KINDERGARTEN
(For Four and Five Year Olds)

Phonics - Bremner-Davis Phonics, Reading with Phonics by Hay and Wingo, Open Court.

Reading - McGuffey's Primer, The Beacon Readers.

Arithmetic - beginning number concepts, addition, subtraction.

Science and Health - nature study, proper habits of health and cleanliness.

Penmanship - manuscript printing.

German - conversation, vocabulary building with pictures.

Art - directed art lessons, crafts, cutting, pasting, etc.

Music - singing, listening to records, rhythms, etc.

Physical Education - organized games, free play.

FIRST THRU SEVENTH GRADE

Phonics Reading - McGuffey's Readers, Open Court Readers, Beacon Readers in First Grade, book reports on assigned books.

Penmanship - Cursive writing begun in the second semester of First Grade.

Spelling - taught phonetically with rules.

English - emphasis on correct written expression, beginning grammar, literature provided in readers and assigned books.

Arithmetic - heavy emphasis on arithmetic operations and mastery of the facts, new math concepts introduced if and when the child can assimilate them

Science and Health - Creation Science Research materials.

Health - Concepts in Science.

German - conversation and vocabulary development, beginning grammar and reading in the Fourth Grade.

Art - directed art lessons, principles of art taught from God-honoring point of view.

Music - singing, music appreciation, study of instruments and music theory.

Physical Education - organized team games: baseball, kickball, etc.

Geography - 3rd Grade - map reading skills.
    4th Grade - World geography.
    5th Grade - World and Western Hemisphere.
    6th Grade - Western Hemisphere.
    7th Grade - Western Hemisphere.

History - 3rd Grade - American History.
    4th Grade - American and California History.
    5th Grade - American and California History.
    6th Grade - World History.
    7th Grade - World History.

UNIFORMS

The children wear uniforms. The girls wear an attractive blue and white plaid jumper and the boys wear navy blue trousers and a white or light blue shirt, the girls a white blouse.

LUNCHES

The children bring their lunches from home. Milk is supplied at school. The price is included in the tuition.

TRANSPORTATION

The school does not provide any transportation, but we do make every effort to cooperate with the parents in helping them to form car pools.

GRADES

Written grade reports are issued four times a year. In most subjects we give numerical grades as well as letter grades to provide the parent with more exact information on the student's progress. Parent-teacher conferences are encouraged any time a problem arises.

STATEMENT OF PRINCIPLES
The Ferndale Board of Education
Ferndale, Michigan
(adopted on August 18, 1958)*

The Board of Education of the Ferndale School District recognizes the need for a clear statement of the aims and practices of our public schools. In assuming responsibility for the school system in these challenging times the Board adopts the following principles and policies as guide posts for the professional conduct of our schools:

1. The principal aim of the schools shall be the development of the minds and the acquisition of knowledge by all children. All other aims, however important and desirable they may appear in themselves, shall be subordinated to this primary aim insofar as the functions of the schools are concerned.

   For the proper understanding of the physical and social world in which we live, a trained mind and a good fundation of factual knowledge are essential for every member of a free and mature society. Every student shall be given the opportunity to achieve these goals. The curriculum and the practices of teaching and counselling shall be so designed as to place the primary emphasis on intellectual development and skills, not overlooking the importance of manual and physical training. Our future citizens should be so educated that they can make informed choices and intelligent decisions in their personal lives, their business, craft or profession, in civic affairs and in the political world, local, national and international.

2. We affirm our belief that, although "Life Adjustment," social adaptation, mental health and similar endeavors are important concepts which should not be violated by a wisely conducted school system, they are not primary goals of our public schools.

   Mature attitudes, tolerance, social understanding and respect for our fellow human beings should be fostered and encouraged by a humane climate in the schools and by the conduct and the example of the teachers. It is questionable, however, whether these desirable attributes can be taught as subjects. Rather they must flow from many sources, especially the home, as well as the church or synagogue, the school and various civic and private organizations. Each of these institutions has an important role in shaping the personality and the social outlook and behavior of the child, a role which the school should support but cannot take over without jeopardizing its primary function. An interest in the child as a whole is laudable but the school does not have the legitimate responsibility for all aspects of child development nor can it deal effectively with the problem of shaping our society except in the specific area of learning. It is true that in bringing together all the children of the district for intramural as well as extracurricular activities, the school automatically becomes an important element in democratic living. However, the specific task of the school in the area of social and personal attitudes of the child is the creation of understanding and knowledge through the study of the humanities — a word most appropriately expressing our purpose of providing humanizing influences — namely through history, government, language and literature, the arts, music and social science.

3. The curriculum will be strengthened by designing a specific program for the elementary schools and one or more programs for the high school which all students can follow. Such programs, supported by appropriate credits and minimum requirements for promotion and graduation, shall be designed to insure a true basic education for every child. This goal cannot be accomplished merely by offering a variety of courses.

Recognizing as a matter of course the differences between individual children with respect to intellectual capacity, maturity, emotional pattern and background, we hold that these differences must not be allowed to interfere with the fundamental education each child receives. Consideration for the individuality of the child cannot obscure the real purpose of the schools, which is to provide a measurable standard of education for all children. Being unable to provide individual tutoring for every child, we must of necessity attempt to find reasonable common denominators. Grouping according to a flexible system, taking into account age, maturity and ability in any given subject, shall be regarded as a desirable practice. In this manner we intend to provide fair opportunity for the gifted student, for the slow learner and for the "average" child. In other words, consideration for the individuality of the child shall be a major concern of every teacher and counsellor and shall determine as far as possible the rate of progress and the quantity of subject matter to be mastered by the individual student, but it shall not affect the basic offerings and the quality of education available to all children.

4. Children, being by definition immature, are not generally equipped to choose subjects, topics, methods or rates of learning or teaching. The teacher shall assume responsibility for planning and teaching the subject matter to be covered in a given period in accordance with an approved outline of study at each grade level.

To relate the contents of a course and the assignments given to the students as much as possible to the interests of the children is obviously desirable. The teacher shall make it his or her business to take the fullest advantage of existing interests, motivations and familiar situations to which the subject under study can be related within the framework of the course of study to be covered. Elevated to the rank of a guiding principle, however, the concern for motivation and "relatedness" defeats the basic purpose of education. The child cannot determine his needs in advance, and the contents of a course may not be initially of interest nor may their usefulness be recognizable to the untrained and inexperienced mind. It is the responsibility of the school, in conformity with Board policy, to determine what should be offered to the students. It is the responsibility of the teacher, by his or her own mastery of the subject, by careful preparation, by the choice of methods and materials, to present the subject in an interesting and stimulating manner. It is the teacher's business to arouse interest even where none may have existed before. To kindle interest and to arouse enthusiasm, to promote a sense of accomplishment — these objectives we consider the essence and the challenge of teaching.

5. Implicit in the foregoing paragraphs is the intent of the Board to have comparable standards of performance and coverage of subjects, grading and promotion throughout the School District.

Within limits, autonomy of the individual schools and teachers is desirable so as to encourage the development of distinctive institutions with close ties to the parents and children in the various areas. However, the desire for autonomy cannot be permitted to extend to the curriculum prescribed by the Board nor to the basic materials and methods employed in teaching. The Board is charged with the responsibility for maintaining standards of education in the Ferndale School District. It cannot effectively do so unless it is assured that a uniform policy will be followed and comparable standards will be observed throughout. On the other hand, the teachers shall be encouraged to go beyond the assignments prescribed by the curriculum both in choice of topics and materials. Also, student participation in determining activities in the classroom shall be encouraged as long as the basic assignments are met.

6. The Board rejects the concept of the core curriculum, integrated studies program, common learnings type of instruction or similar programs as the basic method of instruction, since this concept tends to minimize subject matter and interfere with the acquisition of accurate information which must precede integration.

The orderly, planned acquisition of knowledge requires some degree of separation of the subject matter to be learned into its component parts. English is not mastered in a course of social studies, nor is mathematics mastered merely because it is used in connection with some other subject or activity. To integrate knowledge an understanding of related subjects after the elements have been conquered is a desirable and logical approach, but such knowledge and understanding must first be acquired in a clear, simple and direct setting. The teaching of clearly identifiable courses is necessary if the Board and the schools are to have effective control over the curriculum This principle need in no way be construed as interfering with the teaching of several subjects during consecutive periods by a qualified teacher.

7. Without exerting undue pressure, the teacher shall have the right to expect each student to work according to his or her ability.

The Board accepts the fact that learning of most of the skills and subjects taught in school requires mental discipline and a serious effort which is not incompatible with enjoyment. It believes that the making of such an effort is in itself a necessary experience, an indispensable part of the process of education which should lead to an appreciation of difficulties to be overcome and to an eventual sense of accomplishment. The systematic use of textbooks and the assignment of a reasonable amount of homework, depending on grade and subject shall be a normal procedure in all schools. The development of good study and work habits shall be a recognizable goal of our schools.

8. The teachers shall be free to encourage and wisely direct competitive efforts by the students, channeling them into productive undertakings and avoiding unfair comparisons.

Children have a natural desire to excel. We regard a wisely guided competitive spirit as wholly desirable in a competitive democracy. A society which confuses democracy with conformity or mediocrity cannot survive. Lack of the wish to excel leads to lack of interest and failure to bring out the full innate ability of the child. The school has an obligation to develop all the talents and skills the country needs in these different times. It shall be the purpose of the schools to arouse in each student the desire to excel or at least do his level best. Grading, examinations and report cards are not in themselves a guarantee that this purpose will be achieved but the Board regards them as essential adjuncts to other teaching methods. These techniques are not intended for punitive purposes but are to be used as a yardstick of accomplishment, a challenge and a means of stimulating effort and interest.

9. The Board recognizes the accomplishments of the Ferndale School District in the field of special education and pledges its support to the continuation of this program.

The needs of handicapped children clearly represent a separate and important problem which must be recognized and supported to the fullest possible extent.

In setting forth these principles, the Board is accepting the responsibility with which it is charged by the Law, namely that of setting a policy which shall be binding on the schools in the district. The implementation and execution of this policy the Board entrusts to the professional staff in the expectation that it will faithfully cooperate in the development of a specific program along the lines presented here. This policy shall be reviewed annually at which time changes may be adopted.

* Used as basis for developing guidelines for Fundamental School in 1976.

A PROPOSAL FOR A FUNDAMENTAL SCHOOL

This school should be made available to families in the District who desire their children to have a fundamental type of education. The basic activities of the Fundamental School will be to:

1. Emphasize instruction in reading, writing, speaking, arithmetic, and the teaching of basic science and cultural subjects.
2. Specify a uniform policy for homework at all levels.
3. Seek to develop efficient study and health habits.
4. Place emphasis on character building, and the teaching of moral principles and common courtesy.
5. Emphasize discipline, respect for authority and patriotism.
6. Have a dress code for students and teachers.

In a number of study sessions we have had input from parents, teachers and educators, both inside and outside the District, and we have discussed this matter with business people. As a result, we have formulated a number of proposals in connection with setting up such a school which we would like to present at this time.

This Fundamental School is not to be considered an exact copy of any other existing fundamental school. A survey of concerned parents, teachers, administrators and taxpayers, both from within and outside the District indicate there is a community need for a particular type of alternative school which will concentrate on the teaching of the three R's and other basic subjects. Without these basic tools of education, students are ill equipped to meet life's daily challenge. Even worse is the plight of college bound students who find themselves in dumbbell classes geared for those seriously lacking in the language arts.

A fundamental school will not be in conflict with any other school. It is designed to be a complement to the present school system. It will be an alternative school.

The "alternative school" is a concept which is sweeping the nation. The idea behind this is that, in a society such as ours, parents should have a choice as to how they want their children educated. We live in a permissive society, and a very large proportion of our youth has been brought up permissively. Regular public schools must handle all types of youngsters. This has meant that regular schools have had to provide a variety of activities other than academic, and they have had to revise discipline and behavior standards accordingly to meet the needs of these young people, hopefully to keep them in school.

Another part of the population, however, a part that is growing and becoming increasingly articulate, desires a more academic and structured type of fundamental education for their children. In many districts at present these people have no choice except to send their children to private schools. In this District an increasing number of children are being sent to private schools and each of them not only deprives the District of ADA money but also takes money out of his parents' pockets for private tuition. In a sense, this is double taxation.

Our objective is not only to get some of these students back into the system, but also to make possible a fundamental education available to those families who cannot afford private schools. We can achieve this by setting up a fundamental school as an alternative school.

In actual practice then we will have two schools, which will have different missions and will fill different needs in the community.

The Fundamental School should not be designed nor should it be intended as a school for the elite — that is, students with high I.Q.'s. On the contrary, the Fundamental School should be designed to teach and train the average student, the student who is *willing to learn and whose parents want him to learn* and develop those skills, disciplines and abilities which are essential to successful living.

There are some kids who are perfectly normal and perfectly capable of learning but lack the ambition. They won't do anything unless they get a kick in the pants. Well, the Fundamental School is designed to administer that kick in the pants — that is, academically. This can only be accomplished by a structured, orderly program. And so — while the students may not be elite when they come into the school, it may be hoped that they will be elite when they get out.

A fundamental education is just as important for Black youngsters as for white youngsters. In fact, statistics show that in Pasadena the success with Black students has been almost phenomenal in their fundamental school — so much so that from recent indications Black parents are very pleased and well satisfied.

The objective of the Fundamental School will be to treat everyone alike, no special privileges, no discrimination, no tokenism. If parents make application and signify willingness to stick by the rules, and the student obeys the regulations, pays attention in class and does his best, that's all we can ask of him. It is certain that there are many, many parents in the District with children who will profit by this type of environment.

Some people feel that the Fundamental School will tend to draw all the good students away from the regular school. This is not likely. Students with high I.Q.'s are usually self-motivated and don't need a structured program. The regular school will be larger, more diverse, freer, with a greater variety of courses. Young people differ. Many simply will not adopt to the highly academic program and the academic work required in the Fundamental School. Parents know best and will make the decisions; and some families, I am sure, will have youngsters in both types of schools.

The proposals we have in connection with the setting up of a fundamental school are as follows and I am sure our membership as well as many others in the community will support these proposals.

Administration. We do not believe any administrative overhead will be necessary. Since attendance at the Fundamental School will be voluntary and at the request of parents, minimal disciplinary problems are anticipated. A maximum of six teachers will be involved on a permanent basis. It is recommended that one of the teachers be appointed as team leader and be made responsible for the coordination that will be necessary between teachers and assisting parents to accomplish the school's objectives. Additional administrative matters should be handled at the District office. As provided in the proposed Handbook, the school, for the most part, within the framework of State and School Board regulations, should be autonomous with control resting in the teaching staff.

Curriculum. There will be but one curriculum designed to accomplish the school's objectives. All students will take the same subjects. Teaching methods and class procedures will be determined by the teaching staff who will consult with parents as outlined in the tentative Handbook. Insofar as teachers will be expected to continuously research, and to follow the most up-to-date and effective teaching methods, as well as to evaluate periodically the learning progress, it is recommended that the school be supplied with a part-time receptionist and stenographer. Other services can also be furnished by the campus office.

The sixth grade curriculum will follow that of the District, which is already set up, using the same textbooks with such minor changes as the teaching staff may decide. There will be emphasis on the three R's.

The curriculum for the seventh and eighth grades will be sequential, covering a two-year course in math, a similar course in English and language usage which will occupy two periods a day; also a two-year course in world science and in world history which will give students an overview of what has happened in the world since its beginning. These are described in greater detail in a handbook.

There are several suggested innovations, one of which is a fifteen-minute interval between classes, long enough to allow students a short game of ping pong, a little basketball, badminton or whatever may catch their fancy. This is suggested by Premack's research in which he discovered that students were more alert and learned better during any period when they could look forward to a pleasurable activity that would immediately follow. This would be advantageous because class periods in the Fundamental School will be strenuous and exacting.

You will also notice in the handbook that the proposed school day is longer with extended snack and lunch periods, during which students can engage in interesting and profitable activity such as games, socializing or study. This was suggested by parents who think students are not kept long enough in school at the present time.

Teaching Staff. The Association has heard from enough teachers presently employed by the District to be assured that enough competent teachers will volunteer to staff the Fundamental School without having to bring anyone in from outside.

Cost. Present estimates are that a fundamental school of the nature and dimensions which we request should not represent any additional cost to the District. Quite possibly it should produce additional revenue for, if the Fundamental School is properly set up and operated, it is bound to attract additional students to the District who otherwise would go to private schools thus increasing ADA income. The ADA allowance per student will follow the students wherever they go, whether to regular school or fundamental school. Since we will utilize classrooms already available within the District, volunteer teachers already on our staff and textbooks available within the District, it is difficult to see where additional cost will be incurred unless a modest amount may be needed to move a portable classroom or two, pay the stenographer and an extra fee to the Team Leader. It should be possible to require parents to transport their own students as they do in private schools, if this is necessary.

PROPOSED PHILOSOPHY OF THE TRADITIONAL MAGNET SCHOOL LOUISIANA

This school shall regard its main function to be the development of each student's basic academic skills. Each child will be expected to develop competence in reading, spelling, elementary mathematics, good English grammar, composition, and penmanship. These main objectives are to be achieved at the earliest grade possible within the framework of a tightly-structured, sequential system of learning. To add interest and to enrich the curriculum, studies in geography, art, music, history, social studies, science, and current events shall be undertaken, but these subjects are to be the "salt and pepper" not the "main dish."

Although the school is not to be considered wedded to any particular method of instruction, the main emphasis is to be drawn from proven, traditional methods. The school will recognize that much of the development of elementary skills requires the use of memorization. Students will be expected to prepare for recitations, sometimes with the help of parents in drilling them at home. Parents are expected to cooperate in seeing that homework assignments are done on time. Competition shall be fostered as a motivational force for the children. A greater emphasis shall be placed upon the development of indepdendence rather than interdependence. Each child can expect to be challenged to the limit of his ability, to do his work promptly, to learn to accept responsibility, and to work against deadlines. These objectives are to be undertaken to the degree that is consistent with the maturity that can be expected from the ages of the children being taught. The school accepts the principle that school should be enjoyable, but the school also believes that each child will find pleasure and enjoyment from his sense of progress and accomplishment.

Each child's progress will be measured against norms for his age group and against his class average. Children who do not achieve normal progress for a given grade level should not expect automatic promotion to the next grade level. Any child whose progress is substantially below that of his peers will be considered for retention and repetition of a grade or for reassignment to another school that better suits his needs.

CURRICULUM

1. A traditional school should present a basic academic education of high quality. All minimal State requirements will be met.
2. There will be a strong emphasis on functional skills, reasoning ability, work and study habits, recall of facts, and traditional values of patriotism, family, courtesy, self-discipline, and good citizenship.
3. Reading, arithmetic, and language are basic.
   a. Reading - basal reading approach; strong emphasis on phonics *and* comprehension; workbooks; a unified basal program throughout school; strong emphasis on library books and home reading assignments.
   b. Arithmetic - importance placed on mastery of basic skills; drill and repetition important; homework expected; metric system to be taught.
   c. Language - emphasis on oral and written skill development; paragraph writing; punctuation; capitalization; parts of speech; outlining; formal grammar in writing and speech; sentence diagramming; spelling and vocabulary study to extend into every academic area.
4. Penmanship, science, social studies, P.E., art and music are also part of this curriculum.
   a. Penmanship - daily practice; *all* work must be neat and legible for acceptance.
   b. Science - unified program throughout school to prevent repetition; emphasis on vocabulary. Demonstrations of experimental method when possible.
   c. Social studies - patriotism stressed in history studies; current events, history, and geography to be studied particularly in upper grades.
   d. P.E. - daily classes for all grades with emphasis on skill development in large and small motor coordination; lifetime sports; calisthenics.
   e. Art - integrated into other subject areas; fundamental drawing skills to be introduced at appropriate age levels.
   f. Music - taught for skill and enjoyment; provide cultural background.
5. Scope and sequence are to be set for each grade giving a unified approach to all major subjects.
6. Areas to be covered must be standard at each grade level, but the teacher may choose her own method of presentation. A teacher is free to teach in her own style, but must stay within the overall framework.
7. Workbooks can be used along with other methods of drill as needed.
8. There must be a good central library as well as a good small library in each classroom. Each class from third grade up shall have its own set of reference books or encyclopedia. Children are to be required to read

and report on at least one library book per week as soon as their reading skills are sufficient.

9. Rules and punishments are to be the same for all. There will be a written policy embracing the policy of the school system and additional specific rules. This policy statement must be made available to parents and must be supported by parents and faculty.

   a. Discipline shall include respect and obedience to all adults, respect for the rights of fellow students, orderliness in classrooms, following directions.

   b. Teachers have authority to mete out discipline. Punishments may include writing lines, going to office, paddling, and staying after school.

10. There will be a uniform policy concerning procedure of giving and returning homework, minimum and maximum amount, and standard manner of assigning grades to homework. All work must be neat and legible to be acceptable.

    a. Parent cooperation is essential with strong followup at home.

    b. Homework is to be given daily except Fridays.

    c. Parent orientation handbook will be prepared and presented at a parent workshop at the beginning of the school year.

11. Standardized tests are to be administered at the beginning and end of each year as one measure of progress. At the beginning of the first academic year a program of accountability and evaluation is to be developed by the school board central staff. Standardized tests are also to be used for diagnostic purposes to help tailor individualized instruction programs. If measurement of a child's educational progress indicates that the pupil is falling short of his educational goals remedial work is to be assigned.

12. Scholastic achievement is to be emphasized and honored, particularly through competitions such as spelling bees, math competitions, etc. Independent achievement rather than group interdependence is to be stressed.

13. There will be no "social promotions."

14. The faculty will determine specific curricula following these general outlines.

ADMISSIONS

1. A selection committee composed of the principal, a community member appointed by the school board, and one member of the school board's central staff will review applicants and make final decisions on individual admission cases, and the initial selection is to be as nearly random a selection as possible from the pool of applicants. Applicants interested in the philosophy of this educational concept will be recruited from all segments of the community.

2. Parents shall be required to make application for admission of their children on a standard form. After admissions are completed the

parents must sign a statement agreeing to certain stipulations before an admission becomes final (attachment 1).

3. Children attending the school already will be given preference for admission the next year. Where practical an attempt will be made to accept all of the children in a particular family if the parents so desire. Vacancies will be filled by the admission committee.

Attachment 1

As the parent(s) of a child enrolled in the traditional magnet school, I hereby agree to:

1. read, initial and return the attached statement of school philosophy, to signify my agreement with same.
2. support both school assignments and discipline by supervising homework or home drills and requiring obedience to school rules. It is clearly understood that the school may (if need be) use corporal punishment, i.e. spanking.
3. abide by the school decision with respect to what constitutes a satisfactory standard of achievement, with the clear understanding that there will be no social problems.
4. allow a fair trial period (the first 9 weeks) before requesting a change of schools on the part of either the school or myself.

_____

Signature of Parent(s)

VIEWING CHARACTER EDUCATION GUIDELINES FOR PERSONNEL OF THE PASADENA UNIFIED SCHOOL DISTRICT
Dr. John Mike Kellner
OBJECTIVES

A. Honesty and fairness
B. Kindness, consideration and assistance to others
C. Faithfulness, loyalty and trustworthiness
D. Self-image
E. Dependability & Punctuality
F. Citizenship
G. Personal Rights
H. Responsibility

Moral education is legal; it is in fact required by law in a number of states. Section 13556.5 of the State of California Education Code reads: *Training of Pupils in Morality and Citizenship* — "Each teacher shall endeavor to impress upon the minds of the pupils the principles of morality, truth, justice, patriotism and a true comprehension of the rights, duties and dignity of American citizenship, including kindness toward domestic pets and the humane treatment of living creatures, to teach them to avoid idleness, profanity and falsehood, and to instruct them in manners and morals and the principles of a free government."

Character is taught, not caught. It modifies behavior to the point that instruction is significantly more productive.

With appropriate character education there has been a reduction in discipline problems. The experience provided in this area of study results in deeper insight into honesty, truthfulness, reliability, justice, kindness, etc.

The teaching of responsibility is a most important task. It can be learned at any age. Developing character in young people is a tough job and one that requires patience, tact and skill.

ONE HUNDRED SUGGESTED CHARACTER EDUCATION IDEAS

The following character education ideas are provided as resource material. They have been compiled from suggestions and proposals submitted by teachers, parents and students. During the past three years these have been used at various grade levels with impressive results.

1. The wise one profits by his own experience; the wiser one as much by the experience of others.
2. Failure occurs only when you fail to keep trying.
3. Sooner or later a busy person learns to write things down. It is the best way to capture things we are apt to forget.
4. In a leadership assignment, how do you know if people are following you?

5. Be able to distinguish between achievement and success.
6. Understand the importance of a sense of humor.
7. With regard to a boring task, how can it be done better?
8. What is the importance of respecting authority?
9. Every disadvantage should be analyzed to find an advantage.
10. In order to like other people you must first like yourself.
11. You must be willing to admit your shortcomings and then correct them with all your might.
12. Make it a point to always be the first to say, "Hello."
13. Aim high. There is plenty of room at the top. It's the bottom that is crowded.
14. How can you make new friends and get people interested in you?
15. What is the difference between experience and theory?
16. Be willing to admit you are wrong.
17. Enthusiasm makes the difference.
18. Try to see yourself as others see you.
19. Ask yourself, "How am I doing?"
20. What is smile power?
21. What is eye power?
22. People remember you for the little things.
23. Whatever you dislike in someone else, be sure the same weakness or fault is not part of you.
24. How you apply yourself today will greatly influence the kind of day you will have tomorrow.
25. A nice person is one who can disagree without being disagreeable.
26. The character you possess is due to your daily thoughts, actions, speech, reputation, etc.
27. Life is not an empty cup, but a measure to be filled.
28. Kindness should be silent.
29. Character is being kind and loyal, patient and strong, winning the right, and defeating the wrong.
30. Character is having faith and morals, feelings and love, and believing that there is someone up above.
31. Character is doing things to help others and things to help you, with some of the things you don't want to do.
32. Character is wanting to do all these things, and to want the happiness that character brings. So have character in every way, and it will help you day by day.
33. What does character education mean to me?
34. One can build character education within themselves.
35. There are a number of ways to build your character. Find the way that you can build yours the best.
36. Character education begins and is built on improving one's self-image.
37. Self-image is a picture or opinion of one's self.
38. Character comprises a person's qualities or traits.

39. Motivation and courage are needed to succeed, have a good life, and feel that one is a worthwhile person.
40. Without courage goals cannot be reached.
41. Happiness bolsters the positive forces and fights defeat and negativism.
42. Enthusiasm without knowledge is like running in the dark.
43. Rewards are usually anti-climatic — the fun is in doing.
44. A successful person is one who goes ahead and does the things the rest of us never quite get around to doing.
45. Think of what others ought to be like, then start being like that yourself.
46. Name three stimulating challenges.
47. The person who tries one more time is never a failure.
48. Anger is often more harmful than the injury that caused it.
49. The goal of criticism is to leave the person with the feeling that he has been helped.
50. What counts is not the number of hours you put in, but what you put in the hours.
51. A mistake is evidence that someone has tried to do something.
52. The way to be happy is to make others happy.
53. It's smart to pick your friends — but not to pieces.
54. The only way to have a friend is to be one.
55. What constitutes good cafeteria manners?
56. A friend is one who comes in when the whole world has gone out.
57. What is the difference between generosity and kindness?
58. How should I plan for experience which relates to leadership?
59. How can a student develop pride in his school, home, community?
60. What can older students do for younger students and what can younger students do for older students?
61. The importance of setting goals for our future.
62. The meaning of respect and trust.
63. What is meant by the understanding of feelings and the causes underlying negative emotions? (Anger, jealousy, lying, stealing, selfishness, ingratitude, disrespect.)
64. Show how you attain a good self-image from the following approaches: personal values and worth, doing things you can be proud of, to be pleased with yourself, doing your best, and acceptance of, and obedience to authority.
65. Guidelines in establishing worthwhile values (friendship, loyalty, promises and trust).
66. Understand the true meaning of each holiday.
67. Suggestions for the achievement of higher grades in citizenship.
68. According to Webster, humility is defined as a state or quality of being humble in spirit, freedom from pride and arrogance, meekness, lowliness of mind, modesty and mildness.
69. The great German poet and statesman, Goethe, wrote, "Talent unfolds itself in solitude, but character is built in the stream of the world."

70. What good did I do yesterday?
71. Half the truth is often a great lie.
72. When you're good to others, you're best to yourself.
73. Character education must be conceived as a "continuous experience of good values." The following words are submitted for a depth study: cooperative, leadership, industry, personal appearance, initiative, honesty, courtesy, reliability, dependability, effort, self-control, conduct, punctuality, obedience and thrift.
74. Characteristics for a good citizen: walks correctly in line, uses his independent study time wisely, is kind to others and respectful of other's rights, pays close attention in class, remembers to bring things back to school, does his homework every night, enters the auditorium quietly and listens carefully, tries even harder on a rainy day to be helpful, has good cafeteria manners, obeys all adults, is never in the building without a pass, takes discipline correctly, picks up paper, never fights, never uses bad language, is honest, is not shy, is trustworthy, keeps his hands to himself, plays correctly, shares and has a good memory.
75. The importance of being on time and punctual.
76. Thomas Paine once said, "Youth is the seedtime of good habits."
77. Explain what is meant by a "place for everything, and everything in its place."
78. What is the difference between industry and frugality?
79. The care and protection of private and public property.
80. Express your plan for successful living.
81. What is the difference between talkers and doers?
82. Explain the meaning of: "We get out what we put in."
83. If one knows of their strengths and weaknesses, how does one go about to bring a change?
84. How do we conquer laziness?
85. The way to preserve freedom is to live it.
86. What is the rationale for a clean campus?
87. Do you know any wise saying?
88. The purpose of education is not the accumulation of information but the development of mental ability.
89. What are the characteristics of good health?
90. What is the difference between honesty and fairness?
91. How can we help the student who is not quiet and polite?
92. Why is it important to be attentive?
93. What are the ways to show appreciation to people who have done something special for you?
94. Think twice before you become involved in the violation of any school rule or regulation.
95. Do something nice for someone, then both of you will enjoy a happier day.
96. Identify examples of pride in the appearance of your school campus.

97. What does character education mean to me?
98. Prepare a character education pledge.
99. When health is lost, something is lost. When character is lost, all is lost.
100. The great hope of America is individual character.

PRIVATE SCHOOL, LOS ANGELES

Phonics. 5-year-olds learn to read in kindergarten. They learn sounds by reading the beautiful handpainted charts and a Phonics Workbook written by their teacher.

McGuffey Readers and Modern Readers. McGuffey Readers are the basic reading textbooks, supplemented by modern phonetic readers. Only the finest children's books are read for comprehension and appreciation. No material with questionable moral content or improper language is used.

Foreign Language. Beginning in kindergarten, the children learn to count to 100 in French and acquire a basic vocabulary. In the elementary grades, additional vocabulary and fluency in conversation is gained. The languages usually offered are French and Spanish.

Accelerated traditional math program. Drills are the keynote to arithmetic facts! Drills are fun, often in the form of races, but always important. Addition and subtraction facts to 20 are learned perfectly, so the answer is automatic. Some second graders are now learning the multiplication facts and processes.

Cursive handwriting begun in first grade. Cursive handwritting includes correct forms of the letters, legibility and ability in reading handwriting.

History and Patriotism. Our glorious heritage of freedom in these United States is emphasized by learning and discussing the important events of history and famous sayings of great Americans. Respect for the flag, our Constitution and other historical documents is taught. The upper grades acquire a detailed knowledge of the basic facts of the U.S. Constitution by a careful study of the "Elementary Catechism of the Constitution."

Geography. The continents, hemispheres, countries, states of Mexico and the United States, the provinces of Canada, plus other important geographical features such as rivers, oceans and mountain ranges are studied.

Spelling. By the end of their kindergarten year, students spell 50 words per week by sound and rule. In the elementary grades, the children learn certain words each week, but are not limited to those words. Second graders spell words taught in other schools in sixth grade.

Creative Writing. All types of creative writing is begun in kindergarten, expanded in each grade, and greatly enjoyed by all the students. Public Speaking is taught in all grades. The children learn self-assurance and poise, and a gradual mastery of the basic rules of elocution.

Science. Science textbooks are used in the upper grades which stress Creation by God, rather than evolution. The perfect order of God's creation is studied by students in the kindergarten and primary grades by an understanding of such wonders as birds, flowers, butterflies, bees, weather, seasons, and many other subjects.

Physical education. Various team sports, exercise, jogging and play skills for various grade levels are taught on a completely fenced football field and play area.

Art. Art appreciation is developed by the analysis of great masterpieces. Practical instruction is given in applied art, pencil drawings, lettering and water colors. Oil painting is offered on request to qualified students.

FUNDAMENTAL SCHOOL PHILOSOPHY JEFFERSON COUNTY, COLORADO

We believe the public schools should offer the tools for mastering systematic, factual and disciplined subject matter with clearly set accomplishment requirements that follow specified sequence of subject matter grade by grade. We believe such a program is necessary to prepare students for successful, consistent step-by-step matriculation and intelligent, responsible citizenship. We believe that treating reading, basic arithmetic, spelling, writing, geography, and history as serious subject matter is valuable academically as well as necessary in training in the concepts of truth, justice and virtue. Certain things in this world are lastingly important and education is to seek out and pursue those values. We also belive in related enrichment programs and creative work by the students *after* achieving a clear understanding of the subject and/or course content. We further believe that letter grades, clearly defined and explained, are a useful means of reporting the strengths and weaknesses to students and parents alike.

We believe that the one-teacher, one-classroom plan at the elementary level gives security to a student, as we believe also that a classroom atmosphere of disciplined order and mutual respect provide the proper setting for a basic education program. One of the teachers expressed another wise viewpoint related to this plan. To have his own students all day, in all classroom circumstances and accomplishments, means that he can know them, love them, be concerned with and for them, and thus fulfill what he believes is an integral part of being a teacher — character guidance as well as academic guidance.

Realistic standardized tests will be given periodically to ascertain the ability and progress of our students. We anticipate that the method of teaching and the challenging content of subject matter will motivate the students to want to succeed.

MARSHALL FUNDAMENTAL HIGH SCHOOL
Verdelle C. Reynolds, Principal
PHILOSOPHY

MARSHALL FUNDAMENTAL HIGH SCHOOL, dedicated to the concepts of scholarship, patriotism, courtesy, respect, responsibility and citizenship, seeks to provide a climate for the development of these ideals. In light of this philosophy, Marshall strives to develop in the student:

1. The highest possible competence in fundamental skills.
2. Growth in citizenship, moral and spiritual values.
3. Responsibility for personal behavior.
4. A spirit of individual achievement and competition.

At Marshall, patriotism is heavily emphasized. It is our belief that the American Heritage should play an important role in education. Marshall teaches its students that at all times they must be ready to support and accept responsibility for the preservation of the ideals upon which our nation was founded.

During the past few years, our nation's eyes have seen a constant decrease in quality education. The time has come to recapture true values in education. Here at Marshall, a new schooling feature has been reborn. We have returned to basic fundamental education.

This highly structured process is producing success not only in the school, but in many other similar fundamental schools across the nation. Committed to fundamental principles, the school operates under a well disciplined environment.

ACADEMIC FOUR YEAR REQUIREMENT, ALL STUDENTS — ENGLISH

ENGLISH

Four year requirement, ALL students
NINETH GRADE
Basic Grammer/Basic Composition
TENTH GRADE
Poetry/Creative Writing
ELEVENTH and TWELFTH GRADES
Four of the following *semester* courses during grades eleven and twelve:
First semester choices
Classical American Literature
Greek Drama/Shakespeare
Journalism/Newspaper
Second Semester Choices
• Advanced Composition/Basic Grammar Review
Speech/Newspaper
British Writers
• Strongly recommended for college bound students
MATH

MATH
NON-COLLEGE BOUND STUDENTS
Two years of math: select two of the following:
Pre-Algebra

Algebra I

Algebra II

Geometry

COLLEGE BOUND STUDENTS

Two years of college prepartory math: select two of the following:

Algebra I

Algebra II

Geometry

*Geometry

*Geometry is strongly recommended for college bound students

**If Pre-Algebra is needed, it may not be included in the two-year requirement

These are merely *requirements.* Additional years may be taken if desired.

SOCIAL STUDIES

Four year requirement, ALL students — No choices

NINTH GRADE

World Geography/California History

TENTH GRADE

World History

ELEVENTH GRADE

United States History

TWELFTH GRADE

U.S. Government/Free Enterprise; Economics

GRADES NINE through TWELVE

Government Fundamentals :(Class and ASB officers only — Taken in addition to regular history class)

Office Practice may not be taken along with this class.

1 semester consumer ed. (to be fulfilled in grades 9-12)

FOREIGN LANGUAGE

Two years of foreign language strongly recommended for ALL students. Required for college bound.

COUSE OFFERINGS

Latin I, II

Spanish I, II, III, IV

French I, II, III, IV

German I, II, III, IV

Under unusual circumstances, non-college bound students *may* satisfy the two year language requirement from the following list:

Typing II

Shorthand

Bookkeeping

Clothing

Shop Classes

Drafting

118

SCIENCE

One year of *Biology* required for all students — may be completed between grades ten and twelve. College-bound 2 years required.

COURSE OFFERINGS

Biology
Chemistry
Physics

BUSINESS

One year of typing strongly suggested for ALL students. May be completed between grades eight and twelve.

COURSE OFFERINGS

Typing I
Typing II
Shorthand
Bookkeeping

MUSIC

Senior High Chorus
Senior High Band/Orchestra

CO-CURRICULA ELECTIVES

A wide range of electives are available such as:

1. Typing
2. Art
3. Music
4. World of Construction
5. Metal Shop
6. Drafting
7. Office Experience

VI
A GUIDE TO STARTING
A FUNDAMENTAL SCHOOL

1. Get involved. Look into your local public schools and attend board of education meetings. Identify the board members who agree with your point of view, and those who don't. Ask questions. Make statements.

2. Organize a group of citizens who are concerned about public education in your community. Find out about upcoming school board elections. Decide upon a course of action. Basically, if your local school board already favors fundamental education, you can begin to plan your school. If not, you must decide whether you choose to run candidates in the next school board election or if you will work through existing channels.

3. If you choose to elect your candidates to the board of education, there are some points to keep in mind:

    a. Become informed about local election rules.

    b. Choose your candidates wisely. Start with a broad-based committee to discuss possible candidates.

    c. Find a capable and experienced campaign manager and plan your campaign strategy carefully.

    d. Select a finance chairman and committee early and put them to work.

    e. Put out a brochure. It should contain fundamental education philosophy and pertinent statistics from your community, which you have researched carefully.

    f. Select a public relations chairman to schedule talks at local clubs, organizations, radio stations, etc. Rehearse before you meet the public. Make contact with local newspapers.

    g. Go to the precincts. Make personal contact with voters. Organize to get people out to vote.

If you choose to work through the existing establishment, be persistent, stick to your guns, and don't be intimidated by the delaying tactics of your opponents.

4. A sympathetic board of education is a major asset when you're trying to start a new public school. As elected officials who represent the State, the board authorizes new schools and makes policy for the district. Initially you must indicate to the board that there is sufficient demand for a fundamental school in your district.

5. Plan your school. Design its organization and how the school will reflect your educational philosophy. Select a site for your school. A school which has been closed because of lack of enrollment is ideal, but also regular schools may be converted into fundamental schools. A compromise is to create a fundamental school within a regular school which works best if there is some physical separation between the two schools.

6. Prepare and distribute a press release giving pertinent information about your proposed school. Then you can send questionnaires to parents of children in your district, who are at the grade levels which will be included in your school. A sample of such a questionnaire follows. Parents may respond to the questionnaire by applying to the school.

7. Select administrators for the school. These should be people who believe strongly in fundamental education and, hopefully, are experienced in the district. Such people can help select faculty. Then you are ready to set up the curriculum, clean and repair the site and select the students. Students may be chosen on a first-come-first-served basis, on the basis of their test scores, in order to make the school representative of the district's achievement level and/or in a way that preserves ethnic balance. Each class must be ability grouped.

8. Open your new fundamental school.

INTEREST QUESTIONNAIRE
THE FUNDAMENTAL SCHOOL

Next year, at the kindergarten through junior high level, a special type of school called Fundamental School is proposed at one or more locations in the district. Some of the features of the Fundamental School are:

1. Emphasis will be on fundamentals — reading, writing, spelling, arithmetic, discipline, respect. Art, music and physical education will also be provided. Skills of basic math, rather than "new math" will be stressed. Reading instruction will employ a rigorous phonics program beginning in kindergarten.

2. Homework will be assigned in each basic subject at every grade level, on a regular basis.

3. Classes will be ability grouped.

4. Letter grades will be given periodically in each of the basic subjects.

5. Strict discipline will be maintained. Paddling and detention are permitted at the discretion of the teacher.

6. Dress and appearance, both for students and teachers, must comply with minimum requirements.

7. High moral standards, respect, courtesy, and patriotism will be emphasized at all grade levels.

8. Transportation will be provided.

Admission to the Fundamental School will be voluntary. There are no minimum ability requirements, but achievement and IQ testing will be performed upon admission and periodically thereafter. Parents or guardians must agree to meet with the teacher as required to discuss the progress of the child.

. . . .

Please fill in the bottom portion of this page and return it promptly if you would like your child to be enrolled in the Fundamental School next year.

PLEASE PRINT

I would like to enroll my child in the Fundamental School next year.

Child's Name _____

Present School _____ Present Grade_____

Home Address _____ Phone_____

Signature of Parent or Guardian _____

HELPFUL ORGANIZATIONS

The following organizations will prove helpful to back-to-basics groups. All are dedicated to improving our educational system.

America's Future, Inc., Textbook Evaluation Committee, 542 Main Street, New Rochelle, New York 10801

Council For Basic Education, 725 Fifteenth Street, N.W., Washington, D.C. 20002

Educational Research Analysts, Box 7518, Longview, Texas 75601

National Association of Professional Educators, 223 Thousand Oaks Boulevard, Suite 425, Thousand Oaks, California 91360

National Educator's Fellowship, Inc., P.O. Box 243, South Pasadena, California 91030

Reading Reform Foundation, 7054 East Indian School Road, Scottsdale, Arizona 85251

Richlore Foundation, P.O. Box 3006, Fullerton, California 92634

SUGGESTED READING

Blumenfeld, Samuel - *The New Illiterates and How You Can Keep Your Child From Being One.* Arlington House, New Rochelle, New York 10801 (1973)

Diehl, Kathryn and Hadenfield, G. K. - *Johnny Still Can't Read But You Can Teach Him At Home.* Cal Industries, 76 Madison Ave., New York (1976)

Dobson, James - *Dare to Discipline.* Tyndale House, Wheaton, Illinois (1973)

Eggerz, Solveig - *Federal Aid For Social Engineering In The Public Schools.* ACU Education and Research Institute, 422 First Street, S.E. Washington, DC 20003 (1976)

Eggerz, Solveig - *Our Public Schools — Control Them If You Can.* Heritage Publishing Co., Milwaukee, Wisconsin 53202 (1973)

Flesch, Rudolf - *Why Johnny Can't Read.* Harper & Row, New York (1955)

Hefley, James C. - *Textbooks on Trial.* Victor Books, Wheaton, Illinois (1976)

Johnson, Mary *Programmed Illiteracy in Our Schools.* Clarity Books, Winnipeg (1970)

Kline, Morris - *Why Johnny Can't Add.* Vintage Books, New York (1974)

Langerton, Edward P. - *The Busing Coverup.* Howard Allen, P.O. Box 76, Cape Canaveral, Florida 32920

Rafferty, Max - *Suffer, Little Children.* Old Greenwich, Conn. (1962)

Rafferty, Max - *What Are They Doing To Your Children.* New American Library, New York (1964)

Rudd, Augustin - *Bending The Twig.* American Book Stratford Press, Inc., New York (1957) (Out of Print)

Vetterli, Richard - *Storming the Citadel: The Fundamental Revolution Against Progressive Education.* Educational Media Press, Box 1852, Costa Mesa, California 92626 (1976)

Wellington, James - *American Education — Its Failure and Future.* Arizona Public Service Co., P.O. Box 21666, Phoenix, Arizona 85036